A CASE OF
DOM PERIGNON

from the Victorian Carriage mystery series

For Sandy

All the best –

ALAN M. PETRILLO

AUGUST WORDS PUBLISHING!

unique books by exceptional authors for select readers

Published by   **August Words Publishing**

www.AugustWordsPublishing.com

www.augustwords.org

Cover design	Cricket Freeman
Book design	Cricket Freeman
Cover photos	Historic images
Author photo	Courtesy of the Author

ISBN: 978-1-942018-10-0

For my wife, Gayle, who always helps keep my feet on the ground when I'm reaching for the stars.

Chapter One

Herbert Bradnum awoke with a start, bolting upright in bed, the sheets tangled around his legs. The lightning left a dull afterglow in the tiny bedroom, yet he could barely see the small bookshelf in the corner. His nightshirt, damp with sweat, stuck to his chest and stomach, and he shivered when the wind banged against the window pane, sending a draft of chilly air past him. The rain could not be far behind now, he thought, and in the next instant, fat drops of wind-driven rain began to flatten themselves against his window, then run in wavy rivulets down to the sill.

He pulled the bedclothes close around him and went to the window, watching the storm unleash itself on the outside world. Bradnum shivered again and hugged the bedclothes tighter. Padding across the room to the washstand, he lit a lamp and peered at the container of Eno's Fruit Salt. The old-time, ever-popular remedy for biliousness, sick headache, constipation, errors in diet, giddiness or gouty poison, according to the label. Well, he thought, I must have at least two of those afflictions. He poured a generous measure into a glass of water, swirled it around, and drank it off in a long draught.

Back in bed he smacked his lips and tried to dispel thoughts of the unfinished cases piled on his desk. He'd get through them, he thought, but only if he didn't die first.

❧

King Edward VII squared his shoulders and stared into the mirror while his valet brushed specs of lint from the back of a pin-striped Saville Row-tailored jacket hanging on the coat tree.

"It's ready, your majesty."

The king turned and held his arms out from his sides, then slid them into the sleeves with a soft rustling sound. He flexed and brought his shirt cuffs popping out of the jacket sleeves, then dropped his arms and studied himself in the mirror. Satisfied with his appearance, Edward nodded to the valet and strode from his dressing room. As he exited the suite, his private secretary fell into step behind him.

"Your majesty, I have a telegram I think you should see. It's quite... unusual."

Edward took the flimsy yellow sheet and squinted at the message.

```
HIS MAJESTY EDWARD VII:

PLAN TO SPEND FOUR WEEKS IN AFRICA
SHOOTING GAME * SHIP STOPS FIRST IN
LIVERPOOL * WOULD LIKE TO ARRANGE MEETING
WITH YOU AND SPEND SEVERAL DAYS IN ENGLAND
* ARRIVAL IN LIVERPOOL SCHEDULED FOR 14
SEPTEMBER 1907 * CAN YOU ACCOMMODATE ME? *

                        THEODORE ROOSEVELT
```

"What do you make of that, Taylor?" the king asked, handing back the flimsy. "The Americans are so damn informal. It sounds as if he's leaning over the back fence and inviting himself for supper."

Edward saw the corners of Taylor's mouth lift, even though the rest of his face remained impassive. "Your majesty must remember that such things are done differently in the colonies."

The king gave a loud snort. "I suppose there's no getting around this visit. He seems to already have made up his mind. See to the arrangements."

Herbert Bradnum straightened and massaged his sore back with both hands. He found traces of footprints outside the broken window, plus the sill was scuffed where the thief had dragged something across it. He looked back through the garden behind Elmfield House to the copse of trees in the near distance. The old manor sat at the north edge of the city and at the very limit of his jurisdiction. As an Inspector in the Hull police force, Bradnum was not required to investigate a run-of-the-mill burglary, but the Chief Constable had thrust this one on him personally because the owner of Elmfield House was none other than J.R. Earle, the owner of Earle's Shipbuilding & Engineering Yard.

Bradnum hated dealing with the toffs from the upper class. They invariably looked down their noses at working men like him and usually harbored unrealistic expectations when it came to handling criminal matters. He shrugged off the thought and trudged around the sandstone-faced manor to the rear entry and then let himself into a small room adjacent to the kitchen. A large, moon-faced woman in cook's garb bustled through a doorway and stopped short on seeing him.

"Ah, madam. Inspector Bradnum," he said, waving his warrant card in her direction. "I'd like to have a look around the room that was broken into. Is it through there?" He pointed through the doorway where she stood.

"Down the hallway and second left."

Outside the indicated room, Bradnum stood for a moment and listened to the sounds in the house. Nothing. Quiet as a graveyard. If sound didn't travel well through Elmfield House, then it was small wonder no one had heard the break-in last night. Inside, he surveyed the desk's opened drawers and the scattered papers on the floor, then stepped to the window the thief had used to cnter.

"I beg your pardon. What do you think you're doing there?" The plummy sounds of upper class diction cut through the stillness.

"Inspector Bradnum," he said, turning to face the tall, thin man standing in the open doorway.

"Well why didn't you announce yourself earlier?"

Bradnum drew a deep breath. "I did so to the housekeeper, and also to the cook back there," He jerked his thumb toward the rear of the house. "And to whom am I speaking?"

"I own this place. J.R. Earle,"

"Ah, Mr. Earle. You are the one who can help here."

"It is not my duty to help the police do their job."

"No sir, it is not. However, if you could examine the desk and table over there, I would be most desirous of knowing what might be missing."

Earle hesitated in the doorway as if considering the request, then strode across the room and sat behind the desk. As he rummaged through the drawers, Bradnum returned to the window and inspected the floor around it.

"This will take me some time, sergeant," Earle said, slamming a drawer shut.

"Of course, sir. Are there any other rooms in the house that show obvious evidence of being entered?"

"I've not been told of any by the staff."

"I'll just have a quick look around to be certain."

"Suit yourself." Earle dismissed him with a wave of his hand.

Bradnum made a complete circuit of the ground floor, and finding nothing amiss, mounted the wide stairway to the first floor. It appeared that nothing had been touched. Ten minutes later, he returned to the study and found Earle staring out the broken window.

"It appears this was the only room that was entered, Mr. Earle. Were you able to determine if anything was taken?"

Earle turned and leaned against the window frame. "Two hundred pounds in cash is missing, all banknotes. And also a gold watch and chain, and two gold rings."

"Anything else?"

"Some personal papers."

Bradnum cocked his head. "Papers? What kind of papers?"

"What the bloody hell does it matter?" Earle exploded. "They were simply some legal papers. It's no concern of yours."

Bradnum pressed his lips together tightly. "All right, sir. I'll need a description of the watch."

"It's an American Waltham. It was my father's."

"We shall do all we can to recover it for you."

"You damn well better," Earle said as he strode from the room.

ॐ

Thomas Taylor glided down the thick carpet in the center of the wide hallway, thinking about the difficulties that the American president's visit would entail for him and the rest of the royal staff. The king would most certainly enjoy himself with the president, Taylor well knew. King Edward was first and foremost a social being, having been reared in privilege and power. But while such access might have turned another person's head toward stiffness and aloofness, the king had a well-earned reputation as a popular royal, one beloved by the people for his good humor toward them and his accessible nature in public.

But that was the difficulty the king's staff would face with Roosevelt's visit, Taylor thought as he entered the Blue Room on the first floor where the appointments staff worked. The American president was very much like the king in terms of popularity and it would be a near-impossible task to suppress the energy of the two of them once they got together in a public arena.

And then there were the security concerns that faced him with the heads of the two most powerful countries in the world together in the same place at the same time. The police forces would be pulling their hair out by the roots once they learned of Roosevelt's visit.

Taylor stepped inside a small office and shut the door behind him. From behind an ornately-carved walnut desk, a diminutive man wearing brass-framed spectacles peered up at him.

"Murphy, I would like a few words with you. I have an assignment that you can assist with."

Brian Murphy stood and made a small bow, indicating a plush chair in front of the desk.

"The king will be entertaining the American president in September for a brief visit while Roosevelt passes through on his way to an African safari. We're to rouse up a bit of pheasant shooting for the two of them, along with several official appearances. Some type of dedication would do nicely, along with a formal dinner." Taylor stood and dropped the telegram on the desk. "Contact the president's staff and get the wheels turning for the visit. Get a schedule of the dates they expect to arrive, how long they intend to be here, and the date of departure."

Taylor paused as Murphy read through the wire.

"Once we have the dates in hand, we can work on filling in the time for Roosevelt and the king. Any questions?"

"None, sir. I shall make contact immediately."

Taylor reached across the desk and took the wire from Murphy's hands. "There's a good lad. Stay sharp on this detail."

ॐ

Teddy Roosevelt paced the perimeter of the Oval Office, hands clasped behind his back, brow furrowed, his gaze fixed on the patterned carpet. As he completed his fourth circuit of the room, a light cough from the doorway distracted him and he glared at the interruption.

"Robert, I asked not to be disturbed until I've worked this out. What is it?"

Robert Wallace, the president's chief of staff, slid into the room, extending a telegraph flimsy.

"Sir, I thought you might like to see some cheery news."

Roosevelt snatched the message and read:

```
MR. PRESIDENT:

I CONSIDER IT AN HONOUR TO HOST YOU IN
SEPTEMBER * MY STAFF WILL CONTACT YOURS
CONCERNING ARRANGEMENTS * PERHAPS YOU'D
LIKE A SPOT OF MOORLAND SHOOTING BEFORE
AFRICAN VISIT? * PHEASANT AND HARE PLENTIFUL
IN AUTUMN * WE CAN WAGER ON THE OUTCOME *

                                    EDWARD VII
```

A grin broke over the president's face. "Pheasant shooting! Not a bad way to spend part of a state visit. And there's the probability of winning a bet from the king. See, Robert, there's a silver lining in every cloud."

"Yes, sir. Shall I get things started on this end?"

"Absolutely. And let's be certain the arrangements aren't bollixed up like that visit to Montreal last year. That was damned embarrassing."

"I'll oversee the preparations myself."

Roosevelt fixed Wallace with a sharp look. "Be sure you do." He gestured toward an armchair. "Sit down, Robert. I'd like to talk to you about this banking issue."

ॐ

"Taylor, tell me again why it is important that I go to Hull for this dedication?"

"Your majesty, the Hull Tramway Company is celebrating the thirtieth anniversary of its founding, and its tenth year of electrification. The firm has purchased the newest model trams available and placed them in service on the city lines. We've had an invitation from one of the directors, Mr. Earle, to have you perform the dedication."

Edward VII leaned back in the armchair and puffed a blue cloud of smoke from his cigar.

"Bigod, old Earle." He stood and paced in front of his aide. "J.R. Earle owns the largest shipbuilding company in Hull, probably on the entire east coast, save for the London trade. And Earle is a dead-on shot when it comes to pheasant."

"Yes sir. I remember the year he shot two dozen brace at the Duke of Pleasanton's country house in Surrey."

"So do I, Taylor. So do I," the king said, slapping his palm with his fingers. "I've a capital idea. "We've invited Roosevelt, or better said, he's invited himself, for a state visit. I've offered pheasant shooting as a diversion. We should have the president come to Hull and help with the dreadful dedication. Then we all can go over to Earle's country house and shoot birds. How does that sound?"

Taylor made notes as the king spoke. "I think your majesty has hit on a splendid idea. By involving the American president, we will give the dedication an added emphasis, which is sure to please the company directors. It also places the president and your majesty at a shooting site that is sure to yield a large amount of birds."

The king's face broke into a wide smile. "See to it, then. And be sure that Earle knows I want to be paired with Roosevelt. The wager, you know."

Taylor bowed lightly toward the king, then left the room to make the arrangements.

ALAN M. PETRILLO

Chapter Two

William Cole struggled to the window and drew back the heavy drapes to reveal a brightening sky littered with deflated clouds, and a wet landscape dotted with dark puddles. He had slept heavily during the night, helped along by a last pint of Tartan lager. Cole stretched and padded softly down the corridor to the bath, where a splash of cold water from the tap brought him fully awake and back in control.

Once dressed, Cole rummaged in the kitchen cupboard for something to eat, but found nothing but a near-empty box of stale biscuits. He ate the two remaining biscuits, then put water on the boil for tea. Five minutes later, a steaming mug of unsweetened tea in hand, he negotiated the stairs to the ground floor and pulled his jacket collar close as he stepped into the chill morning air.

Westbourne Street already was full of activity, with other early-rising workmen walking the pavements toward jobs at the Kingston Saw Mill or the Eastern Fish Curing Sheds. On the cobblestoned street, fume-belching gasoline-driven trucks jockeyed for position with lumbering, horse-drawn wagons, such that a pedestrian made nearly as good time as the vehicles.

A quarter-mile walk brought Cole to the Hessle Road Tramway Depot, where he had worked as a tram driver since the electrification and expansion of Hull's tram lines ten years earlier. He paid a young boy two pence for a copy of the *News Herald*, then tucked the paper under his arm and headed into the tram shed, a vast building that took up a space larger than a football pitch and occupied much of the block along Hessle Road and Liverpool Street.

Inside, the clamor of metal parts being smashed together rose from the rear of the building as Cole stopped to admire the triple rows of Preston trams standing on the tracks in the main bay of the depot.

"Billy, wot are you gawkin' at?"

Cole turned to see George McBirnie grinning at him. McBirnie was a former tram driver who had made the switch to tram mechanic.

"Admiring the trams. They look so graceful when they're all lined up like that." He gestured toward the silent trams.

McBirnie shook his head from side to side. "I'll not understand what goes on between your ears. Isn't it enough that we have to drive them all day?"

Cole smiled. "That's the best part."

☙

Richard Purling shook himself like a wet dog, trying to wriggle into a sweater that had shrunk a size too small for him. When he finally struggled into it, he smoothed it over his shoulders, then stood in front of a stained mirror and wet his hand to plaster his unruly hair flat. Most mornings, no matter what measures Purling took, once his hair dried, it reverted to its chaotic state. He glowered at his reflection, then puffed out his cheeks and exhaled a sharp breath. Blimey, I look a fright, he said aloud.

Locking his flat door, Purling used care in negotiating the creaking staircase, well aware of the weak boards in the middle of the stair. Outside, he quickly walked to the corner and turned onto West Dock Street, heading toward its intersection with the Neptune Street Branch of the London & North Eastern Railway. He could smell the dead fish and garbage that inhabited the mooring areas of St. Andrew's Dock and the adjacent Billingsgate Fish Market. As he drew opposite the market, the odor assaulted his nostrils more heavily, even though he was nearly two hundred yards away.

Purling quickened his stride and turned up Manchester Street, and within minutes was at the rear entrance of the Hessle Road Tramway Depot. He nodded to the elderly guard at the wire gate and hurried through a dark doorway into the engineering area, where he would spend his entire day, save a break for lunch, diagnosing problems with the electric trams.

"Morning, Richard. Rough night?" The question came from an engineer seated on a metal stool, toying with a copper-coiled rotor.

"Bullock, you old fool. Why don't you mind your own business?"

Tom Bullock straightened on the stool and smiled. "Ever the cheery fellow, eh Richard? There's a pot of coffee on the boil at the back. Hot water next to it if you prefer a cuppa." Bullock inclined his head toward a workbench at the back of the workspace. "Help yourself, as usual."

Purling brushed past the man and pulled a chipped porcelain mug from the back of a workbench, then blew into its interior before pouring coffee for himself. Sipping the hot liquid, he screwed up his face. "Bloody awful."

"You don't have to drink it then, do you?" Getting no answer, Bullock changed subjects. "Have you had a look at the newspaper this morning? It says King Edward is going to dedicate the new line going up Prince's Avenue into Park Ward. There's to be a ribbon cutting because of the tramway's tenth anniversary of electrification."

"Edward the Seventh," Purling said in a sing-song voice. "He may be king but it's a damned foolish waste of his time and energy. The managers and owners will be fawning all over him, trying to curry favor."

"It's not often that we see the king. The last visit he made here was six years ago in ought-one, the year he was crowned.

Purling fixed Bullock with a baleful look. "It can only mean more work for us, in any case."

"Speaking of more work, we've two more trams down with motor difficulties. I was thinking you could have a look at them, as you're so good with the motors."

"You were thinking wrong, then." Purling said. "I've got work to do on the electric generating unit out back. It's been acting up, again."

Bullock shrugged and returned his attention to the rotor. "Suit yourself. But you're the best with the motors."

❧

Brian Murphy sat with his knees and feet together at the end of a wooden bench in Mayfair Square, his hands folded in his lap. The brisk wind threatened to blow his hat off, and he had to retain it with a restraining hand several times. After fifteen minutes, he was joined on the other end of the bench by a red-bearded man with a florid complexion. For several minutes the man said nothing, and only looked around the square at the birds flitting among the trees. Finally he spoke.

"I watched to see you weren't followed. You should be aware of your surroundings and the people near you."

Murphy noticed the man had not looked at him, but spoken straight ahead as if to the square itself.

"I am always careful when it comes to the cause. Your superiors should know that by now."

The man slowly turned his head and stared at Murphy. "No one is contesting your loyalty. Your wire said the issue was urgent. That's why they sent me. Now what is it?"

"What am I to call you?"

"Is that important?"

"It is, to me."

The man hesitated. "You can call me Loughrey. Shamus Loughrey."

Murphy studied Loughrey for a few moments before slipping a folded sheet of paper from his pocket. He pushed it across the bench toward Loughrey, who snatched it up and stuffed it into his coat pocket.

"Now give me the gist of what's being planned."

Murphy looked left and right before speaking. Then he quickly outlined the details that had been developed for Roosevelt's visit.

When Murphy finished, Loughrey pursed his lips and stretched his leg in front of him. He stared straight ahead.

"Do you need any other information?" Murphy asked.

"As usual, any additional details that pertain to the project should be given to us as quickly as possible. Especially any information about locations and times. Do you understand?"

Murphy looked directly into Loughrey's dead-fish eyes and nodded. He couldn't seem to make his mouth work.

෨

"Well that's finished." Roosevelt stood and dusted the thighs of his trousers as if he had been engaged in some dirty business. "Robert, you always have sound advice for me when I need it."

Wallace smiled and nodded to the president, but said nothing.

"Now tell me about the king. What's he like?"

"As you might imagine, Mr. President. He rules the British Empire and thus has subjects all over the world."

"No, no. What I mean is what's he like as a man? Any likes or dislikes that you're aware of?"

Wallace sat back in the plush sofa and let his head thump gently against the silk brocade. "Yes sir, the king has plenty of likes. As the eldest son of Queen Victoria and Prince Albert, he held the title of Prince of Wales. He was quite spoiled as a child, although that seems not to have affected his personality adversely. The king is revered by his subjects and well respected in foreign countries. The French are especially fond of him. He has a way of cutting through the diplomatic niceties of foreign visits and coming off as a likeable fellow. But one doesn't expect that quality in royalty, it seems. Still, Edward has foiled his critics by being a king beloved by the people, both at home and abroad."

"I could use some of that likeability here in the states with Congress."

"Well put, Mr. President." A thin smile broke over Wallace's face. "As to what the king likes, he's especially fond of shooting, as you are aware. He's also keen on clothes and haberdashery, as well as social events and parties. And good conversation is said to be a personal favorite of his. On the dislikes side of the matter, I'm afraid I have nothing to offer."

"You've done well. Look a little further into what he doesn't like. I wouldn't want to offend him in any way. Meanwhile, let's plan some type of elegant party for the king while we're in England. We're to be in the north, right? Liverpool's our landfall?"

Wallace nodded.

Roosevelt leaped out of his chair and strode around the room. "Capital! We'll throw a reception for the king. What's the protocol for something like this? Should it be before or after he entertains me?"

"I'll have to check on that, sir. I honestly don't know."

"It's not often that you own up to that Robert," Roosevelt said, cracking a smile. "So we'll shoot some pheasant, have a party, do an official engagement or two with the king, then it's off to Africa for the safari."

"Yes sir. We'll have to work out the details for the end of the trip. Perhaps the king's people can suggest a likely point of departure for Africa."

"Work it all out now, Robert. He's going to be mighty unhappy after I win the wager on shooting pheasants."

Wallace stifled a smile. "Of course, Mr. President. I'll see to it."

≥

Richard Purling shut the heavy wooden door to the electric generation shed and stared into the gloom at the hulking machinery. Satisfied he was alone, he fumbled along the wall until his hand brushed the metal conduit, then traced it down to the light switch. The illumination from the naked electric lights hanging from the high wooden ceiling threw sharp shadows on the twin generating motors that sat side-by-side on the raised concrete floor. Purling gazed along the length of the nearest motor, marveling at the intellect of the man who designed the twenty-foot long behemoth. With its flat gray paint scheme, the motor looked like a giant steel drum sliced along its entire length and laid with its open end down. Heavy steel reinforcing beams, mated to the unit's end curves, gave the impression of a closed archway. A series of pipes snaked into the back of the motor, while heavy cabling, shielded in dense rubber cladding, emerged from the top of the unit. The cabling ran to insulators on a steel frame that led through the side of the building to a heavy wooden tower outside. The second motor was a twin of the first, with its cabling exiting the opposite wall.

Purling ran his hand over the cool steel of the nearest motor and drew a deep breath. As he stood staring at the motor, the door banged behind him and a harsh voice called.

"Purling, what are ye standin' about for, ye bloody buggar. Get to work or ye'll be out with the rest of the ne'er-do-wells. What's the difficulty here?"

Purling cringed at the sound of the manager's voice, but forced himself to reply calmly.

"The number one motor's been acting temperamental, Mr. Gooding. Her wattage readings have been fluctuating widely.

"Well what are ye gawkin' at? Fix the bloody thing!"

Purling drew a deep breath. "I was about to test its output when you arrived." He pointedly left the "sir" off his reply.

Gooding stared hard at Purling, his eyes forming narrow slits in the still-gloomy shed. "Get on with it. Ye knows we have not time to waste." He turned and left the shed.

Purling looked down at his clenched fists, his knuckles white with stress. Slowly, he opened his hands and flexed his fingers. "Bloody fool," he said aloud. "Doesn't know a spot about motors. He'd be lost without me."

Then he stroked the motor's flank again. "Time to get you set up properly. We'll teach that arse a lesson he'll not soon forget."

Chapter Three

Shamus Loughrey sat motionless in a booth at the back of the Crowing Cock public house in Carr Lane, a block west of Hull City Hall, his left hand wrapped around a pint mug of Guinness. The post-work crowd had filled the Crowing Cock to the breaking point, so that thirsty patrons had taken to standing on the pavement outside the public house, taking their drinks, and their leisure there. Loughrey's eyes seemed never at rest, continually scanning the room.

He shut his eyes momentarily when the pub door opened and emitted a rectangle of light that briefly shone into the dim interior of the place, but as quickly was extinguished when the newcomer shut the heavy door. As Loughrey's eyes adjusted to the renewed dimness, he watched the man he knew as William Gallagher thread his way through the throng to the publican at the bar and then be served. Lord knows if that's his actual name, Loughrey mused. Most of the higher-up types in the IRA had aliases.

Gallagher stretched to the left and right, peering around the bodies pressed against the bar and when Gallagher spotted him, Loughrey picked up two mugs and made his way to a corner booth.

"The saints watch over you," Loughrey said, raising his glass.

Gallagher, a beefy man with an almost non-existent neck, nodded and drank, spilling ale down his chin and onto his jacket. He wiped the wet spot vigorously, seemingly unaware of Loughrey's gaze. When he looked into Loughrey's eyes, Loughrey knew better than to comment about the ale.

"You have something for us?"

A small smiled played at the corners of Loughrey's mouth. "That I have. With the good lord's help and the cooperation of a lackey in the king's appointments section, I've learned the American president will visit the king in September for a shooting holiday before Roosevelt ships out to Africa for a safari. The appointments staff also has been delegated to come up with appropriate public appearances for the two of them." Loughrey leaned back in the booth and sipped his ale. "Something of interest to you, perhaps?"

Gallagher drank and then wiped a thin film of ale from his lips. "Do you know where the public appearances will be held?"

"Not yet. But our friend in the appointments office will continue giving us information."

"The shooting holiday. Where?"

"It's to be at J.R. Earle's estate."

Gallagher drank again and pulled his hand across his mouth. "That might prove to be a possibility for us. What news do you have about how Roosevelt will arrive and depart?"

"Nothing at the moment. The arrival is sure to be a heavily promoted and guarded event, I expect. We might have an easier time at getting to the man during one of the events, or perhaps when he is scheduled to leave the country. But we don't know from which port he'll sail."

Gallagher laughed aloud before draining the contents of his glass. "We'll see how long the fellow remains president when we are through."

౨

Albert Leake shuffled through the doorway of the main police station, scratching his chin as he entered the reception room. He eyed the row of wooden benches against the wall, which were filled with a wild-looking assortment of men and women, two of whom sat manacled to bench posts. He crossed the dull wooden floor to a high bench presided over by a diminutive policeman whose head barely showed above its top. Leake stood in front of the bench for a minute before the officer acknowledged him.

"Constable, I'm looking for the policeman in charge of the Earle burglary investigation."

"And who might you be?"

"Albert Leake from the *Hull Graphic*."

The policeman looked him up and down before replying.

"Have a seat over there and wait." He gestured toward the benches along the wall.

Leake moved to the left of the benches and leaned against the drab-painted wall. Ten minutes later, the constable waved him through the doorway behind the counter.

"Ask for Inspector Bradnum," he said.

Leake passed through a busy room filled with policemen working at desks and tables or talking together in small groups. A smooth-faced policeman pointed him to the Inspector's office, where the door was ajar. Leake rapped twice on the wooden doorframe.

"Ah, Mr. Leake; come in. Take a seat, please. I am Inspector Bradnum. What may I do for you?"

Bradnum sat behind a battered desk whose top was littered with papers, bound books, manacles, a truncheon and two badly-stained teacups. His round face was impassive, as if he were watching a dull cricket match.

"I've come about the burglary at Elmfield House. I am told that J.R. Earle lost a considerable sum of money, along with other important items," Leake said.

Bradnum sat stone silent for a half minute. At first, Leake thought the Inspector must be hard of hearing, but quickly changed his mind on hearing Bradnum's response.

"Say, are you not the chap who the other reporters call 'Leaky? How did you come by that name?"

A flush of red spread across Leake's cheeks.

"That's . . . that is not pertincnt here, Inspector."

"Humor me, then. Exchange of information, if you get my drift."

Leake eyed the detective warily, as if a snake might pop out of his pocket at any moment. Finally, he relented.

"If you must know, it was an accident. I had a small bottle of gin in my trouser pocket during a football match. Some shoving started off to the side of me and I became caught up in it. I was pushed to the ground and the bottle broke, soaking my trouser leg. My mates thought it was uproariously funny. They called me Leaky from then on."

A wide grin spread across Bradnum's face as he leaped to his feet.

"Waste of good gin, wasn't it? Never mind," Bradnum said, waving his hand. "You'll want the details on the Earle case. Not much to tell at the moment. A burglar entered the house some time during the dark hours last night. Entry was made through the study window and an amount of cash, jewelry and some papers were taken."

Leake wrote in a small, unruled notebook as Bradnum spoke.

"How much cash?"

"200 quid."

"What kind of jewelry was taken?"

"An American-made Waltham watch, originally owned by Earle's father, along with several other pieces — two rings, a gold watch chain and a gold fob."

"What about the papers. What were they? Important in some way?"

"We have not yet been advised by Mr. Earle about them. We shall know more soon."

Leake opened his mouth to ask another question, then reconsidered. There was a brief silence before he asked, "Is there anything else you can tell me?"

"We think the burglary was the work of a lone man."

"What leads you to that conclusion?"

Bradnum moved to the side of the desk and sat on its corner.

"There are boot prints in the soft ground under the window and small scrapes on the window sill. In addition, only one room was entered."

"I don't understand that last bit," Leake said.

"Bradnum looked at him for a long moment before replying.

"Two burglars most certainly would have entered more rooms and probably drawn attention to themselves inside the house. And one hardly needs two people to burgle a single study. Plus, we would have found a second set of footprints outside and more scrapes on the sill. No, it was one man, alright. You mark me."

Leake smiled and closed his notebook.

"Thank you, Inspector. I would like to check back with you to see how the case progresses."

"By all means, do so, Leaky," Bradnum said, extending his arm to show Leake toward the door. "We are always most pleased to talk to the members of the press." "The smile was still plastered on the detective's face.

As he left the building, Leake wondered who had gotten the best of that exchange of information.

మ

William Cole looked back along the tram's side to be sure all the passengers had boarded, then eased the drive lever forward so the tram picked up speed. He piloted one of Hull Tramway Company's newest acquisitions, a Preston Class double-deck tram. Inside her bright, glistening metal body, she could comfortably seat 20 people on each deck, and many more could be crammed into her aisles, rear stairway, and front and rear platforms. Cole breathed a silent thanks to the company bureaucrat who purchased the Preston, because the tram featured the latest closed-front design, which meant he wouldn't be exposed to the elements. Earlier trams had been of similar design, but had open fronts where the driver sat, meaning that in inclement weather the operator often had a face full of snow, sleet, rain or wind, depending on the time of year. Cole made a mental note to be nicer to the men in the purchasing department the next time he was around them.

As the tram drifted into the long sweeping turn on Charlotte Street just north of the Queen's Dock, Cole was startled to see another tram slewed across the tracks at a forty-five-degree angle at the top of the curve. He decreased power and applied the brakes, stopping his tram fifty feet from the accident. The other tram's front wheels were completely off the tracks, having gouged twin trails over the cobblestones.

"Wot's the difficulty? Why are we stopping here?" came a voice from the rear of his tram.

Cole set the brake and turned to the passengers. "Please stay aboard, ladies and gentlemen. There's a blockage up ahead and I'm going to see if we can pass by."

Cole stepped down from the platform and walked forward, leaving the babble of voices behind him, although he could see many of his passengers hanging out of open windows, trying to get a better look at the cause of the delay. As he approached the front of the disabled tram, Cole recognized the driver standing at the kerbstone.

"Willy, what the hell's happened here?"

Willy Devlin looked at Cole and shook his head. "Damned if I know. One minute I were toolin' round the curve nice as can be, and then, sudden-like, the tram jumps the tracks and decides to go off on her own. I were lucky that me speed were slow or someone might have got hurt."

Cole looked at the front of Devlin's tram, within a foot of touching the front window of Brooksbank and Company warehouse agents. Another few feet and the office manager might have had an exceptionally difficult day, Cole thought.

"Do you know what caused the derailment?" Cole asked.

"Nay, I haven't looked yet."

Cole walked around the rear of the tram, past the crowd that had gathered to watch how the ungainly tram would be coaxed back onto the tracks. As he came up the left side, he ducked down under the bodywork, then emerged with two blocks of wood.

"Willy, come look at this."

"What is it?"

"Oak blocks, cut to fit the gap alongside the track. I saw more under the tram. They must have been placed on the curve where the outward stress would be the greatest on the tram. When your tram hit the blocks, the wheels rode up and over them, and continued on straight off the tracks."

Cole held up the two blocks, turning them back and forth so Devlin could see the gouges made by the tram's steel wheels.

"Who'd be evil enough to do such a thing?"

"A good question. One that we should put to the police."

Within a minute, a long-faced constable appeared at the front of the stricken tram. "Who's responsible for this? Where's the driver?"

"That'd be me," Willie said.

"You've got to shift that tram. It's blocking the street."

Cole could see Willie begin to fume and stepped in front of him.

"Constable, you might want to look at this," he said, holding out the blocks of wood. "I found them on the track under the tram. It looks as if someone intentionally derailed the tram."

The constable pushed his helmet back on his head and turned a piece of oak over in his hand. "The tram hit this and went off the track? Show me where it happened."

Cole led the constable to the side of the tram as Willie began offloading the passengers.

"Over there." Cole pointed to a dim area under the tram. "There are more blocks like these."

The constable disappeared under the tram body, only to emerge a half-minute later with three more oak blocks in his hands.

"Someone went to a good deal of trouble to derail this tram," Cole said.

The constable examined the wood more closely. "That they did. And the Chief Constable will want to know who and why."

❧

Herbert Bradnum stepped back from the facade of the Brooksbank office and bent at the waist to peer under the derailed tram. Far up on the cobblestones under the front of the vehicle he could see two more blocks of wood like the ones the constable had handed him.

"Constable, duck under there and retrieve those blocks," he said, pointing into the shadows.

"Me, sir?"

Bradnum looked around. "You don't see any other constables here, do you?"

The long-faced constable dropped onto his hands and knees, then his belly, and scrabbled forward under the tram. A half minute later he emerged, the front of his uniform dirty, but the two blocks in his hand.

Bradnum glanced at the wood pieces, then placed them in his jacket pocket.

"Mr. Devlin, a moment of your time."

Devlin, who stood smoking a hand-rolled cigarette alongside the derailed tram, stepped forward.

"What can you tell me about the state of the tracks before the accident?" Bradnum asked.

"I already told the constable what I saw."

"Be a good chap and tell me, then."

Devlin gave him a fish-eyed look, and then scratched his head. "Twertn't nothing out of the ordinary, sir. Around the curve I comes, heading along Charlotte Street nice as you please. The next moment, there's a bloody great screech as the tram comes off the rails and skitters across the stones, heading straight for Brooksbank's." Devlin gestured toward the warehouse office.

"Did you see anyone near the tracks, perhaps to the side of the street opposite where you finished up?"

"Nay, I can't say as I did. Me hands was full smashing on the brakes to try to stop the bloody tram. I wasn't lookin' much anywhere but at that building getting closer and closer to my face."

Bradnum watched as Devlin wiped droplets of sweat from his brow. "Thank you, Mr. Devlin. That will be all for now. I suggest that you might want to sit down for a spell to calm yourself.

As Devlin wandered toward a pub in the next block, Bradnum slipped along the side of the disabled tram and moved toward Cole's new tram, which still stood in the middle of the road. Cole, leaning against the front of the tram, nodded as the detective came up and identified himself. Bradnum listened intently as Cole gave an account of his conversation with Devlin.

"I don't suppose you saw anyone suspicious in the area, did you?"

"Suspicious? In what way?"

"Someone who looked out of place, like he didn't belong here."

Cole pulled at his upper lip and shook his head. "No. No one like that."

Bradnum sighed and turned back toward the stricken tram as a grizzled old man led a team of brawny horses toward him. Some things never change, Bradnum thought. The trams may be electrified, but the casualty service is still provided by animals.

Chapter Four

"Mr. President, there's a wire of interest on the corner of your desk," Wallace said as Roosevelt strode into the Oval Office. "It's from the king."

"Capital!" Roosevelt said, rubbing his hands together. "What does he say? He's not backing out of the wager, is he?"

"No sir. I think you'll be pleased with his response."

Roosevelt picked up the flimsy and read.

```
MR PRESIDENT:

MY STAFF BEGINNING ARRANGEMENTS FOR YOUR
VISIT * HAVE A DEDICATION CEREMONY IN HULL
I WOULD LIKE YOU TO HELP WITH * WE CAN
SHOOT AT ELMFIELD HOUSE, J R EARLE'S
ESTATE FOR A DAY OR TWO BEFORE OUR
PRESENCE REQUIRED IN HULL * THE WAGER IS
STILL ON * WHAT SHALL WE SHOOT FOR? * A
CASE OF DOM PERIGNON PERHAPS? *

                              EDWARD VII
```

Roosevelt paced the room behind his desk, his hand pulling at his jaw.

"Dom Perignon is what he wants to bet, eh? Robert, what the devil does a case of Dom Perignon cost? Never mind. Confirm the wager and wire the king that I like my champagne chilled to the bone."

Roosevelt stopped pacing and shot Wallace a big grin. "Go on, Robert," he said, waving his hand. "Get it done."

೨

Richard Purling pushed open the door of the Trident Public House and stood in the entrance, scanning the room. Seeing McBirnie standing at the far end of the mahogany bar, he strode around a throng of noisy workmen, jostling one man's elbow in passing.

"You bloody bloke, watch what you're doing."

Purling stopped in mid-stride and turned toward the man, clenching his fists. Then, as the man's drinking partners clustered around them, anticipating an altercation, he relaxed.

"My mistake," Purling said. "No offense."

The man nodded at him as the group of drinkers whooped and laughed.

"What was that about?" McBirnie asked.

"Nothing that can't be settled at a later time."

Purling ordered a pint and dropped a coin on the bar to pay for it. When the publican put the pint mug in front of him, Purling took a long draught before turning back to McBirnie.

"Are you still working on the motor in Preston 105?"

McBirnie shifted his position. "Aye. The electricals are all burnt out inside. Some of them was as crisp as black toast. I thought I found the source of the problem, but it turned out to be a false lead."

Purling nodded, but said nothing.

"If you could find some time to look at it tomorrow, I'd be appreciative, Richard. Gooding has been after me all week about working faster. I swear that man will push me to the limit one day."

A sly smile crept across Purling's face. "Is that so? Gooding is on your arse too?"

"Aye, practically all the time. He's always wanting everything repaired faster and faster. That's no way to do the work."

Purling sipped the Newcastle brown ale "You're spot on there," he said. "Just the other day Gooding chewed on my arse when I was working in the electric gencrating shed. The damn dolt knows nothing about working with the motors. He only parrots what Earle tells him and that's nothing but claptrap."

"What does Earle have to do with the work in the shop?"

"It's not only the work in the shop. The man controls the entire tramway and all its workers. He's the bloody managing director of the tram company, as if owning the big shipyard wasn't enough to keep him busy."

"So Gooding gets his marching orders from Earle? I'll be damned. Small wonder that things aren't working right at the depot. It's Earle messing about in matters that he should keep his hands out of, eh?"

"Someone should teach those two a lesson." Purling tilted his head and stared hard at McBirnie. "That's what I think."

McBirnie clucked his tongue. "Aye, I suppose you're right."

Purling raised his pint mug in a toast. "To comeuppance. May those that deserve it, get it."

McBirnie nodded and then drank in response.

31

❧

Inspector Bradnum walked through the doors of the main entrance of the Hull Tramway Depot, wincing at the harsh sound screeching metal that emanated from the workshops behind the offices. He planted his elbows on the high counter that screened a stout, gray-haired woman from the reception area.

"Inspector Herbert Bradnum to see Mr. John Gooding." He fixed the woman with a bland smile.

"Mr. Gooding is working on an important project and cannot be disturbed," the sour-faced woman responded.

The smile left Bradnum's face. "I would suggest you get yourself out of that comfortable chair and tell Mr. Gooding that the Hull police are here to question him and if he is not comfortable doing it now, in this place, then I can certainly make it much more uncomfortable for him at the Police Station."

The woman's face froze and she quickly disappeared through a doorway behind her desk.

Bradnum leaned on the counter and belched noisily. Damn, he thought, I never should have taken the Dinneford's Magnesia so soon after the Fruit Salt. Should have given it time to work.

Within a minute, a beefy red-faced man with thinning hair burst through the door.

"What's all this about?" he began. "Who do you think you are?"

"As I told your secretary, I am Inspector Herbert Bradnum and I am here to talk with you about the sabotage you experienced on the tram line yesterday."

Gooding visibly relaxed and turned toward the inner door. "Come along and we can talk in my office."

Gooding's office was a tightly-packed cubicle with shelving along two walls holding an assortment of books, manuals and bound reports. A desk was shoehorned into one corner of the room, opposite which stood a straight-backed chair and a small table piled high with papers.

"Have a seat, Inspector." Gooding gestured around the room. "As you can see, I am busy, so I would hope you'll not waste my time."

Bradnum cleared his throat and forced a smile onto his face. "You are well aware of the facts of the case involving the derailment of your tram yesterday, are you not?"

Gooding nodded and Bradnum continued. "One of the avenues that we are pursuing in this case is one our American friends might call an 'inside job.' I would like to talk with you about any disgruntled employees you might have on your staff."

Gooding leaped to his feet. "Disgruntled employees! The whole bloody place is shot through with the disgruntled, disaffected and indifferent. Most of the staff seems to have some axe to grind with the company."

Bradnum leaned back in the chair and it creaked and groaned.

"Could you be a bit more specific in terms of names?"

"I have a half-dozen for starters. There's Williams and Basel, Jessup and McBirnie, Stout and Purling. Does that help?"

"It is a start, Mr. Gooding. Are all these individuals employed in the same positions within the company?"

"They are drivers and mechanics, the lot of them. I can give you a list of their names and positions."

"That would be most helpful, especially if you could include their addresses."

Gooding went to the door of his office and bellowed for his secretary, who came rushing along the corridor.

"Give the inspector what he requires," he said.

&

Samuel Hind stepped off the westbound tram and hurried along Daltry Street as fast as his arthritic legs would carry him. The Public Baths had recently continued to stay open through the early evening hours, allowing tradesmen like Hind the opportunity to avail themselves of the curative effects of a good soak. Hind had injured his back during the Boer War and had been unceremoniously discharged from service as unfit for duty. Back in Hull, he returned to the only trade he knew, paperhanging. But the continual stretching and ladder work took a toll on his already-injured back and Hind could only find relief in the Pubic Baths.

Hind slowed in front of a row of nondescript terrace houses where the lighting was much dimmer than that nearer the corner with Hessle Road. As he passed a narrow alleyway between two terraces, a muscular arm shot out from the gloom and encircled his neck, dragging him back against the building. Hind struggled against the man choking off his breath, and kicked back at his attacker's legs, causing a momentary release in the pressure on his neck. But in the next instant, something soft yet heavy crashed into Hind's temple, and he crumpled to the ground in a heap.

He opened an eye and looked up through a haze of blood to see a heavily-built man with a whiskered face peering at him. Before Hind passed out, he heard the man say, "Stay off the trams if ye want to be healthy."

&

Inspector Bradnum walked slowly past the club entrance in the Hedon Road, glancing over his shoulder at a pair of sailors overtaking him. His stomach gurgled, almost as a reminder of the reason that he had come to this place. The neighborhood wasn't one of Hull's better ones because of its location in the Drypool Ward near the Victoria Dock. The streets around the club were crowded with sawmills, timber yards, an iron foundry, old warehouses, a railway siding goods shed, rundown wooden houses and dilapidated shops. Stopping in front of a gated yard two doors away from the club, Bradnum let the sailors pass and then returned to the club entrance. It was not so much a club, Bradnum knew, although Hull city records classified it as such, as much as it was a haven for drinkers, opium smokers and whores.

The Oriental Club's entryway was a red-painted door festooned with tattered gold and silver-colored garlands tacked to it. Bradnum pushed the heavy door open and a bell tinkled, sounding again as he shut it. The entry room was quiet, with only two old men sleeping on wooden planks stretched between two small barrels. They snored loudly, and one of them threatened to topple off the narrow plank to which he clung.

Bradnum pulled his pocket watch out and checked the time — near midnight — and moved through a beaded doorway into a dimly-lit, smoke-filled room, oppressive with the heavy scent of opium. He glanced at the still forms of men and women lounging in doll's poses against two of the room's walls, their eyes closed and heads lolling on their chests or shoulders.

As Bradnum studied the closest of the women, a slender Chinese man of indeterminate age slipped through an open doorway. He bowed when he saw Bradnum and said in halting English, "Ah. It you. You come for more?" The Chinese made a rubbing motion over his stomach.

"The same as last time."

Bradnum dropped coins into the Chinese's outstretched palm and the man turned to wordlessly disappear into a back room. He returned within a minute and handed Bradnum a handful of twisted papers, each about the length of a cigarette, but markedly narrower.

"One a time. No cheat."

Bradnum couldn't help but grin. "I remember. No cheating. Only take one at a time."

"Very powerful. Too much make ill." The Chinese man bowed and then disappeared into the back again.

Bradnum stuffed the opium into his pocket and turned for the door. At least he would be able to quell the pains in his stomach for a while, he thought.

Chapter Five

J. R. Earle leaned back in the upholstered chair at the head of the long dining table and stretched. The cook had just brought his breakfast — kippered herring, oatmeal, two soft-boiled eggs each in its own egg cup, dry toast, black currant jam and coffee. A copy of the *Hull Graphic* lay on the right of the table and Earle picked up the tabloid and scanned the headlines.

Nothing of interest, he thought as his gaze wandered over the front page. Turning inside, a headline caught his eye.

ELMFIELD HOUSE BURLGARY PERPETRATOR UNKNOWN;
VALUABLES, IMPORTANT PAPERS STOLEN

by Albert Leak
Hull Graphic Reporter

A large amount of cash, gold jewelry and important papers were stolen from Elmfield House, the estate of shipyard magnate J. R. Earle, during the night Tuesday last.

Hull police report that £200 sterling was taken from Mr. Earle's study, along with an American-made Waltham pocket watch, its gold chain and gold fob, as well as two gold rings embedded with precious stones. The Waltham pocket watch was reported to be especially sentimental to Mr. Earle, as it had belonged to his late father.

Inspector Herbert Bradnum said that it appears only a single burglar was at work on that night, which he deduced from the scuff marks on the window sill through which the burglar made his entry, as well as the single set of footprints below the window. The inspector also made the observation that more than one burglar would certainly have attacked more than the single room, the study, that was ransacked.

No suspects have been apprehended in the case as of this time.

Mr. Earle also is well-known in Hull as the managing director of the Hull Tramway Company, which at present is undergoing some measure of labor strife with its tram drivers and mechanics. It is rumored that some type of action is possible on the part of the drivers and mechanics, especially if the Hull Tramway Company does not accede to the workers' repeated requests to speak about reputed difficult working conditions.

"What rubbish!"

Earle hurled the paper half the length of the walnut table before it separated into individual sheets and floated down like large white birds, littering the polished oak flooring.

"The bloody *Graphic* will pay dearly for that story," he said to the empty room. "I'll not be slandered in my own city's newspaper."

❧

William Gallagher leaned back in the corner booth at the rear of the bar room in the Shepherd's Rest, surveying the crowded room through squinting eyes. When the street door opened and he saw the pair of small men enter the room, he sat straighter and pulled in a deep breath. He watched as they threaded their way through the pub, parting the crowd as if Moses himself had stepped into the room to do it for them.

The larger of the two men, but not by much, sat first and looked Gallagher directly in the eyes. "God bless all here," he said loudly enough to be heard by the patrons in the adjacent booths.

Gallagher raised his glass. "And to you also."

The man who had spoken, Patrick Sweeney, slid along the booth to make room for his partner, David McCafferty. Gallagher held his breath as the two stared him down for several uncomfortable moments before McCafferty spoke.

"Here now, William. You're sitting there with a cool pint of Guinness while the two of us are thirsty from our trip." The smile on his face broadened and he raised his arm, attracting the attention of a freckle-faced barmaid. "Two more pints of Guinness and another for our good friend." He indicated Gallagher, hunched on the other side of the table.

When the barmaid left, McCafferty turned to Gallagher and the smile was gone from his face. "What have you learned for us, William?"

Gallagher took a deep breath. "We have a man placed in London, Shamus Loughrey, who has connections with an appointments secretary to the king. The information Loughrey passed along is that the American president, Roosevelt, will visit the king for a shooting holiday and ceremonial duties in Hull during mid-September." Gallagher tried to sit up straighter, but McCafferty's piercing stare made him feel as if his back were made of jelly. Gallagher glanced at Sweeney and found the man's face a stone mask.

McCafferty angled his head to look at Sweeney, and then focused back on Gallagher. "The actual dates?"

"We know that Roosevelt will arrive in Liverpool on the fourteenth of September. But that's the only firm date that we have now. The appointments secretary told Loughrey that it would be natural for the president to spend the night in Liverpool before traveling to Hull to meet with the king. He expects Roosevelt to travel by train, probably in a special car. The arrangements are yet to be made, but Loughrey will be apprised when they are done."

"And that is all?"

"There's a bit more. Roosevelt is a keen hunter and shooter. He's challenged the king to a pheasant shoot. They plan to shoot at J.R. Earle's estate in Hull. At this point we are unsure if the shoot will take place before the ceremonial dinner that the king and Roosevelt will celebrate."

A thin smile played across McCafferty lips. He took a large draught of the Guinness and set the glass down hard. Flecks of foam dotted the corners of his mouth.

"We shall have to arrange for a special reception for the American president. After all, he agrees with the king in standing in the way of Irish freedom. Perhaps we can persuade him and the rest of the Americans that we are serious in our cause."

Sweeney, who had yet to utter a word, leaned across the table and crumpled Gallagher's jacket lapels in a rough-edged hand, pulling him tightly against the edge of the rough table.

"This is important to us, Boyo. Be sure that you get the right information. Impress upon Mr. Loughrey how keen I am to learn the proper details."

Sweeney, slowly pushed Gallagher back from the table and smoothed out his lapels. Sweeney's gaze on Gallagher never flickered.

Gallagher nodded dumbly, his voice gone.

Sweeney and McCafferty drained the contents of their glasses and left the pub, while Gallagher watched with his heart thudding in his chest.

❧

Inspector Bradnum sniffed deeply and pulled at his nose to stifle the beginnings of a sneeze. The room he sat in was cramped and cluttered, filled with an almost unimaginable assortment of broken furniture, piles of used lumber, boxes of useless metal fittings and crumpled papers. He shifted in the chair and its limbs squeaked in protest.

"Now Mr..." Bradnum consulted his notebook, "Mr. Hind. Please tell me what happened on Daltry Street last night."

Hind blinked slowly, as if the light was too bright for him. A red-stained bandage was wound around the top of his head.

"I likes to use the Public Baths off Hessle Road from time to time. I was walking along Daltry Street toward them, fixin' to have a right proper soak, when some buggar jumped out of an alley and grabbed me."

"Did you see the person who grabbed you."

"Nay; he snatched me from behind and tried to choke me. I got in some strong kicks against his legs and he released me. That's me Army training, ye see." Hind nodded and waited, as if for some kind of approval.

"Continue, please."

"I was about to give him a thrashin' when he smacks me in the head with a short black stick. It was sort of soft, but heavy, if you know what I mean."

"I do. Our American friends call such a weapon a 'cosh.' What happened then?"

"Well, I fell down and blood was flowin' down me face. But I did get a look at the bugger afore I blacked out."

"Can you describe him?"

"Aye. A man with a dark face."

Bradnum waited for Hind to continue, but the man sat there with a stupid look on his face.

"That is your entire description of your assailant?"

"I did have blood in me eyes."

"Ah, yes," Bradnum said, closing his notebook. "And then you blacked out."

"That's it exactly."

Bradnum stood to leave the stuffy room.

"There is one other thing," Hind said. "The man told me to 'Stay off the trams if ye want to be healthy.' That's what he said. Exactly. What do ye think it means?"

Bradnum pulled his hand over his mouth and clucked his lips. "Damned if I know, Mr. Hind. But I intend to find out."

ॐ

Albert Leake edged along the side of the building, taking care to keep out of sight of the entrance to the tramway depot. He had watched the main entryway of the depot for an hour that evening and noted nothing out of the ordinary. The rear entry of the depot held little promise in Leake's mind, but he felt he had to at least spend the time watching to be able to say that he had reviewed all the possibilities for his article. Leake poked his head around the corner again and peered at the rear entry as two workmen emerged through the large doors. He could see that there was some kind of animosity between the two of them from their deportment and the antagonistic way in which they carried themselves.

Leake watched as the two men stopped outside in the yard and stood nearly toe to toe, arguing. He strained to hear what the men were saying but was too far away to discern anything but snatches of words.

Suddenly, the smaller of the two stiffened his arms and shoved the other man, pushing him into a pile of metal parts on the side of the yard. The larger man got up rubbing his head and swung a fist at the smaller man, who ducked. Within moments, the two had grappled and fallen to the ground.

Seconds later another pair of workmen emerged from the rear entryway and ran toward the fighting men, catching hold of them and pulling them apart.

The only thing Leake heard clearly from his distant hiding place was the smaller man shouting, "I'll kill you," to the larger man.

Roosevelt sighted along the twin barrels of the Parker 12-gauge shotgun at a volume of Plato's "Republic" on the top shelf of a bookcase across the room. "Pow," he mouthed, seeing an imaginary pheasant dropping from the sky. He cocked his head at the sound of tapping at the door and smiled as Wallace slipped into the room.

"What a wonderful shotgun Parker makes," he said, holding the gun at arm's length. "Look at those lines, Robert. They're classic. I think Parker's guns rival the best that

England has to offer. I'll wager I'll beat the king with my Parker against his Purdey."

"You're well aware, Mr. President, that I would never bet against you. Nor would I hazard a wager with you."

Roosevelt burst out in a guffaw and clapped Wallace on the shoulder.

"Always quick with the proper answer, Robert. And what news do you have for me?"

"We've made arrangement for the shooting party to take place at Elmfield House outside of Hull. That's the ancestral estate of J. R. Earle. He owns a large shipbuilding company in Hull and also is the director of the city's tram company. He's quite a keen sportsman, so I'm told."

"Capital! Is he a betting man?"

"Does the sun rise in the east?" A thin smile creased Wallace's face.

"Don't you see the irony in the situation, Robert. I have the opportunity to win a wager not only with the king of England, but also one of the peers of the realm."

Roosevelt raised the Parker again and swung it through the room, following another imaginary pheasant.

"Mr. President, if I may continue."

"Yes, of course."

"You arrive in Liverpool on September 14 and spend the night at the Metropole Hotel. An entire floor has been allocated to you and those traveling with you. The next day you will travel by special train from Lime Street Station to Hull, where you will be met at Paragon Station by the mayor. After some formalities, we'll get you to the Grosvenor Hotel, where we have another floor allocated to us."

Wallace looked down at his notes and continued. "The following morning, the sixteenth, you'll motor to Elmfield House on the outskirts of Hull for two days of pheasant shooting. I expect we may be able to manage some hare shooting as well. Accommodations have been arranged for you and the staff at Elmfield House, with J.R. Earle as your host."

He pulled a deep breath and flipped a few pages in his notebook. "On the eighteenth you'll attend the anniversary dedication of a tram station or some such thing with the king, and then attend a state dinner that evening. The next evening we will host a reception for the king and his court at the Grosvenor Hotel. We leave England via the *Majestic* from Hull docks on the twentieth for Africa."

"Robert, I am amazed that you are able to put together so much activity in so brief a span of time. I truly am amazed. And grateful."

"As always, sir, it is a pleasure."

"The only pleasure I'm looking forward to is winning that wager from the king," Roosevelt said, laying the Parker on his desk. "That and taking some money from Earle too."

&

Patrick Sweeney spat into the dirt and then rubbed the spot with the toe of his boot, gouging a furrow a foot long. He spat again and looked down the road at the distant figure walking toward them.

"He's late again. Saints save us, we seem to be waiting for him all the time."

David McCafferty peered sideways at him. "What put the nettles in your bum today?"

"It's not only today. He expects because he does unpleasant work for us he's entitled to special consideration. Remember the last time we negotiated with him. We nearly had a punch-up."

"Better you save your vitriol for the Brits. Remember what this is all about."

"Aye, I am well aware of what it's about. Just you remember I told you he's trouble for us. Sean goes off on his own and doesn't follow the instructions he's given. Nothing but trouble. And it will come back to haunt us, mark me."

"At least hear what he has to say."

Sweeney grunted and spat again. "That I'll do."

He looked down the street and watched as the slim red-headed man approached them, and then passed them by without a word. Suddenly, the lanky man spun on the balls of his feet and turned to face the two Irishman, grinning broadly.

"Jesus, Mary and Joseph, I nearly didn't see the two of you lounging there in the shadows of the pub, what with your short statures and all." He smiled even wider.

Sweeney began to respond, but McCafferty held up a hand.

"Patrick, I'll deal with this." To the red-head he said, "Respect, Sean. It's often said you lack respect."

"Only because there is no one in the organization who commands my respect." The smile was gone from Sean's face and a hard line now defined his mouth, as if it were cut from stone. "Your message said you have a job for me. Is it in London?"

Sweeney took the opportunity to respond. "We have some reservations about your effectiveness. That last bit of work you did for us turned out very messy."

"What did you expect," Sean said, his voice rising and causing a passing couple to look at him in alarm. "You bleedin' buggars aren't leaders. You're no better than dustmen."

Sweeney clenched his fists and pushed past McCafferty, who tried to cut him off. Sweeney squared his stance in front of Sean and looked him square in the eyes. The two stood face to face, unblinking for ten seconds, before Sweeney said in a low voice, "We won't be needin' your services, Boyo. Be on your way."

Sean held Sweeney's gaze for a few more seconds, and after casting a disgusted look at McCafferty, walked away down the street.

"That altercation leaves us with a wee bit of a problem, Patrick."

"Nay, it does not."

"You have a solution?"

"Aye. I'll do the job myself."

McCafferty's eyes widened. "I don't think that's the wisest course to take, Patrick. Think about how exposed you'll be in doing this. You've not done this sort of thing in some time. We can find someone else to do it."

"Nay, we won't. I'm as good today as I was ten years ago when I was snapping arms and shooting villains. I'll take Sean's place. The American president will never know what happened to him. We'll bring the Irish in America onto our side against the bloody Brits."

McCafferty shuddered. "Let's get a pint of Guinness. I think you should take some time to think this through."

"I've done with thinkin'. It's now time for doin'."

Chapter Six

Inspector Bradnum watched as the Number 7 tram trundled along the tracks on George Street where they passed Grimston Street, three blocks from the police station. The first report of an incident on the tramway had been filed three months previously and the problems had only grown more severe during that time. First there had been the incidents of derailed trams crashing into buildings and injuring passengers, due chiefly to a series of oak blocks, cut to fit the grooves between the tracks and paving stones, and obviously intended to do damage to life, limb and property.

The ensuring weeks had seen escalating difficulties on the tram line. A passenger who exited a late-evening tram near the Turkish Baths was accosted with the admonition to stay off the trams. Bradnum had taken the man's statement, but could not piece together enough information to bring a suspect to the bar. Then there had been the stoning incidents, where tram passengers in the central section of the city had been pelted with rocks as they departed a tram. No one had seen the stone thrower, yet the incident took place in broad daylight. Bradnum wondered about the audacity of the perpetrator, risking identification if he were seen or even possibly being caught in the act.

And what statement was a villain trying to make by stoning tram passengers, Bradnum mused. Was he so dissatisfied with the tram service that he resorted to violence in order to make his point? Perhaps he was some sort of maniac who could not control his emotions. Bradnum wiped his forehead with a heavy hand and looked up Grimston Street toward the station. He should be getting back. He took this brief constitutional to clear his mind and try to put a different face on this confusing case, but nothing seemed much clearer to him.

The tramway situation calmed down after the rock throwing incident, only to boil over again when two unattended trams were set afire. The trams, the newer Preston models, had stood apart from the ranks of the others in the rear yard of the Tramway Depot, awaiting movement into the work shed for servicing. Seemingly in the blink of an eye, for no one at the depot professed to witness any unusual activity, the pair of Prestons, standing side-by-side on adjacent tracks, were found fully ablaze from one end to the other. By the time the fire brigade arrived to extinguish the flames, the trams had burned down to their trucks.

Bradnum turned to head back to the station and in doing so bumped against a thin, bent-over old man, nearly knocking him down. Bradnum grabbed for the man's arm and kept him from falling, though the old man's knees buckled for a moment.

"Pardon me. I didn't see you. Are you hurt?"

The small man peered up at Bradnum and squinted. "Is that you, Bert Bradnum? By Jove, it is." The man's face was split by a smile, showing a missing tooth in the top row.

"Chief Inspector Dewson. I hardly recognized you. I heard you had moved to the south of England to get more sun."

Dewson's smile turned devilish. "I try to be where people think I'm not. It was a technique I used when I was on the force and one that you would do well to use." He poked a bony finger at Bradnum's chest.

"Yes sir, a worthwhile suggestion. The old place hasn't been the same since you pensioned off."

"What in bloody hell are you doing standing around on street corners when you should be off solving crimes? The smile had not left Dewson's face.

"One of those cases with an unusual set of circumstances has me flummoxed. I thought a change of scene might help me sort it out, but it has not."

Dewson laid a finger alongside his mouth and struck a pose. "Well, lad, I find myself at loose ends at the moment. The public houses are open now. Stand me to a pint and tell me the tale. I may have an idea you can use."

Why not, Bradnum thought. The chief inspector had one of the keenest minds in the East Riding when he was on the force.

"Any particular kind of ale you'd prefer?" he asked.

The chief inspector started walking down the street. "We might try more than one if your story is long enough. Try to make it long, eh?"

&

"Leaky, come in here for a moment. I should like a word."

Albert Leake looked up from the paper he was studying and squinted at the dwarfish figure of his editor, Samuel Owst, standing in the doorway.

"What news on the king's visit with Roosevelt at the end of the week?"

"Roosevelt is expected to arrive by ship at Liverpool tomorrow afternoon and will spend the night in the Metropole. We have a correspondent who will wire us details of his arrival at the dock and also at the hotel."

Leake paused in case Owst wanted to ask a question, but none was forthcoming.

"The next day a special express will convey Roosevelt and his entourage on the Liverpool and Manchester line straight across the country to Hull. The king's private secretary, Thomas Taylor, will lead the delegation to welcome the president at Paragon Station. The king and the president will meet later in the evening at a private supper at the Grosvenor Hotel."

"What have you learned of the shooting party to be given by J. R. Earle?"

"King Edward and President Roosevelt will travel to Elmfield House and remain there as Earle's guests for the following two days. There is talk of a large wager between the king and Roosevelt concerning the number pheasant each expects to bag."

"Who is the better shot?"

"The king has been practically raised with a shotgun in his hands since he was a youngster, and he is no stranger to pheasant shooting. But Roosevelt has the reputation of being a keen sportsman and an excellent wing shot. I am told that many of our citizens are laying wagers of their own."

"On whom?"

"The money is on the king, although Roosevelt appears to have some support. Perhaps it is due to the odds. The king is favored, two to one."

"Home country favorite no doubt. From what I have read of Roosevelt, one should never underestimate him." Owst stretched and linked his fingers being his head. "After the shooting?"

"The king is scheduled to perform a ceremonial dedication of the Hull Tramway Company's tenth anniversary of electrification. That is scheduled for the Saturday of Roosevelt's visit and both the king and the president will perform the ceremonial duties. The king especially asked that Roosevelt be included."

"Jolly big of him, eh?"

Leake studied Owst's face for a trace of humor, but knew that the editor had a reputation for possessing a lack of it.

"I expect that with the president in town, it was nearly impossible for the king to exclude him. In any event, it is a ceremonial event they must endure as royalty and politicians must do. The two of them have a private supper scheduled for that evening. Roosevelt leaves the next day for Africa."

"Directly from Hull?"

"Yes, sir. A steamer, the *Majestic,* will be sitting alongside Riverside Quay to take the president south to his African safari. It's said he's headed to Kenya for lion and buffalo."

"Well he certainly won't find such creatures here in Hull. It's as quiet and dreary as place as any in England. Nothing ever happens in Hull."

❧

"Two pints of Whitbread," Bradnum said, and dug in his waistcoat pocket for coins with which to pay the landlord. The Queen's Dock public house was a decrepit timber building on the north side of Dock Street, facing the huge area for which it was named. Warehouses and timber yards lined the quarter-mile-long docking area and mooring posts sprouted along its edge like mushrooms after a damp spring. Bradnum hefted the two pints and edged past knots of early-midday drinkers, arriving at a small table where Dewson lounged in a ladder-back chair.

"To your health, Chief Inspector." Bradnum raised his glass and took a long draught.

Dewson wiped flecks of foam from his lips. "This tramway case you're investigating; tell me about it."

Bradnum took a long drink of ale before launching into his involvement in the case. Ten minutes later, he finished his story, but not before the inspector's glass was empty.

"I could do with another."

Bradnum fetched two more pints.

"The way I see it, lad, there are several directions for you to take. But the one with the best probability of giving you a payoff is to look inside."

"Inside? I don't understand."

"Sure you do, lad. Inside. Someone inside the company is behind these incidents."

"All of them? That hardly seems likely. And I've looked into the backgrounds of several employees that the managing director said were outspoken concerning the tramway company. I found nothing."

"Then perhaps you didn't look deeply enough to find something."

Bradnum sat silently, trying to decide whether the old man was insulting him or was simply too frank for his own good. Then he remembered a cold night on the docks years ago, guarding a warehouse of valuables with one of the old hands from the station. The old boy had spoken of the chief inspector, who, he said, always spoke his mind and invariably was right in his assessment. That's what had garnered him the best case-solving reputation in the entire East Riding.

"You are suggesting that I somehow missed some important detail in investigating these individuals?"

"Lad, I am suggesting that things is never what they appear to be. There always is something else happening that we're not aware of. Your job is to figure out what that something is." Dewson drained off half of his ale in a single pull. He smacked his lips when he finished. "Damn, I like a good ale."

Bradnum couldn't help smiling. "Let's assume that you're correct. That means I have to review all those interviews and begin digging deeper."

"Aye. And I would look a little more closely at that burglary at Earle's place. A bit coincidental, don't you think?"

Bradnum had not thought it coincidental, but he was not about to admit it to the chief inspector. "In what way?"

"You have this series of unusual events targeting the tram company, its trams and passengers. Concurrently, a burglary is perpetrated at the home of the chief director of the tramway company. Valuables are stolen from Elmfield House, as well as some private papers that J. R. Earle will not discuss with anyone. Suspicious, you must agree."

"You believe there is a link between J. R. Earle and a tramway employee who is disgruntled to the point of violence?"

Aye, lad. I'm not only suggesting; I am telling you that's where you'll find your villain."

❧

Teddy Roosevelt grabbed the ship's rail and leaned out from the upper deck of the *S.S. Ohio,* the turbine-powered steamship that had carried him across the Atlantic in near record time, owing to favorable winds and more favorable weather. He wavered at the rail as the ship bumped against the wharf fenders, pushed into place bow first by a snout-nosed tug.

Turning to his chief of staff, Roosevelt flashed a toothy grin. "And so the adventure begins."

Wallace inclined his head to the side. "Please remember, Mr. President, that this not entirely a holiday trip. You have important ceremonial duties ahead of you."

The grin was still on Roosevelt's face. "Robert, you worry too much. Of course I shall attend to the ceremonial duties. God knows I've done it enough in my political lifetime. But what I'm looking forward to is bagging more pheasant than the king and taking possession of that case of champagne from him." Roosevelt's expression changed to serious. "It's not that I want the champagne itself, though we'll have a grand time with it. The issue is more primeval than that, Robert. It's what I felt down in Mexico with the Rough Riders. It's taking the measure of a man, and beating him." Roosevelt grinned again, more widely this time. "Let's get off this tub and have a bit of fun at the Metropole."

Bradnum grimaced as he swallowed the thick liquid. He screwed up his face and shuddered as the mouthful of Dinneford's Magnesia slid down his throat, defying him to describe its taste. Tilting the bottle a bit, he reread its label. The Universal Remedy for Acidity of the Stomach, Headache, Heartburn, Indigestion, Sour Eructations and Bilious Affections. He had no idea what those last two ailments were, but because the other four beset him regularly, he was certain he must be afflicted by those two also. He returned the bottle to its place in the bottom desk drawer as Constable James Glew tapped on the doorframe.

"You wanted to s-s-see me, Inspector?"

Bradnum grabbed his hat from atop a pile of papers and came around the side of his desk. "You've read the interview reports on the tramway cases?"

"Yes, s-s-sir. An interesting lot."

Bradnum stopped in mid-stride. "In what way?"

"Well s-s-sir, what s-s-struck me most was the escalating level of violence against anyone associated with the tram s-s-system."

"Stand at ease, Glew. You've nothing to fear from me."

Bradnum could see the constable was nervous in his presence, probably because of the stuttering impediment that had earned him the nickname of Stuck-like Glue. The other constables in the station used it to haze him regularly, which only compounded his stuttering problem. From Bradnum's perspective, Glew's handicap grew worse when he was flustered, but he had a sharper mind for police work than most of those hectoring him.

"Now that you have a flavor of the case, you can accompany me and assist in re-interviewing some of those tramway employees who were on the manager's questionable list."

"Do you expect them to tell different stories, sir?"

Bradnum jammed his hat on his head. "What I expect is one of them will tell us different lies. We have to figure out which one is lying and what those lies are. Now let's get along."

∂

The Pease Street Reading Rooms lay only four blocks away from the main entrance of Hull's Paragon Station, surrounded by a fenced plot of spiky grass growing under elderly plane and elm trees. After arriving on the 2:32 express from London's King's Cross, Gallagher headed for the quiet facility run by St. Luke's Church as a library and reference room for those unable or unwilling to use the Hull Museum's Grand Library. William Gallagher stopped at the entrance and dropped to one knee to tie his boot, and at the same time glanced along the way he had come for a sign of someone following him. There was none.

Inside, he signed into the reading room's roster with a false name and made his way along a dim corridor into the main reading room. Suffused with light from floor to ceiling windows on its south side, the reading room proved to be a stark contrast to the entrance and hallway leading to it. The rectangular room contained eight rectangular oak tables, each complimented by four solid-backed oak chairs. Two reading lamps were arranged down the center of each of the tables.

Gallagher chose an unoccupied table in the far corner of the room and sat with his back close to the angle formed by the two walls of books. Within minutes of his entry into the room, Patrick Sweeney appeared in main doorway, standing stock still, scanning the room with a slow-moving gaze. He looked over Gallagher and continue his scan, and only moved to Gallagher's table after he had apparently satisfied himself about the secure state of the room.

"God bless all here," he said, his gaze level with Gallagher's. "And how does life find you, William?"

"What the good Lord doesn't provide, we find for ourselves. Life is about making choices, isn't it Patrick."

Sweeney leaned back in the chair, lifting the two front legs from the ground and fixed Gallagher with a hard stare. "And have you made the proper choices in life, William."

Gallagher hesitated. He always felt uncomfortable around Sweeney, as if some tragedy was about to happen around him. Being uncomfortable was tolerable, but the truth was he was afraid of Sweeney. Afraid of him, and of his reputation."

"You should know I always have the best interests of the cause foremost in mind, Patrick. I would never betray the cause."

"Interesting that you should use the word, 'betray.' Are you trying to tell me something without saying it?"

"Not at all," Gallagher said, a bit too quickly. "The difficulty is that this Roosevelt predicament is a bit over the top, don't you think?"

A slow smile played across Sweeney's lips and he wiped it away with his hand. "One of the keys to our success with the British will be to involve the Americans by enlisting them on behalf of the cause. Many Irish in America already send dollars back to the old country to help us. What we intend is an event that will cause the average American to notice and take our side against the Brits."

"I have no quarrel with enticing the Americans to help us. But the method that we're using, threatening the American president..." Gallagher's voice trailed off. "I'm not sure it is the right way."

Sweeney leaned across the table and put a surprisingly muscular hand on Gallagher's forearm and squeezed hard. "You should leave the strategy to me and McCafferty. Now tell me more about Elmfield House and how we'll be able to get onto the grounds."

For the next fifteen minutes, Gallagher talked about J. R. Earle and his manor home, Elmfield House, where the king and the president were scheduled to shoot pheasant. Gallagher had walked the perimeter of the grounds and knew the best access points for Sweeney and his accomplices. He told Sweeney all the details, and drew a sketch of the property on a small piece of paper that he drew from his pocket. When he was finished, he sat back, a sheen of perspiration on his brow.

"Now that wasn't so difficult, was it William?"

"Don't mock me, Patrick. I am doing my best."

"I know you are," Sweeney said, patting Gallagher on the shoulder. "The sad part of this whole interview is that we may never need to act on this information."

"What do you mean?"

"Only that we have two men in Liverpool right now, intending on dealing with the American president. They're both good, trustworthy men. We may not need to implement the Elmfield House plan at all, if they succeed."

Gallagher covered his mouth with his hand to hide his surprise.

"That's it, then. William. You have done well. Let's walk down to the Botanic Hotel Public House by the station and have a drink. My treat."

Gallagher could only nod as he stood to accompany Sweeney out of the reading rooms.

Chapter Seven

Michael O'Brien and Peter Duffy stood shoulder-to-shoulder at the edge of the crowd jamming the pavement in front of the main entrance to the Metropole Hotel. There was an expectant hum in the air, as if a swarm of bees hovered over that part of the street. When a murmur went up from the crowd, Duffy, who stood a whisker over six feet tall, stood on his tiptoes and peered down the road.

"There's a big saloon car slowing down in front of the hotel," he said to O'Brien, who at five foot four inches tall would have needed a small ladder to see over the top of the crowd. "Now a footman has come around and opened the door. There's some tout getting out. Wait now. Yes, yes. The next fellow is the president."

As Theodore Roosevelt stepped from the rear of the touring car, a ragged cheer began at one end of the mass of people and made its way across the crowd like a wave breaking on a shoreline before melting into a singular loud chorus of voices. Many of the onlookers applauded Roosevelt as he strode down a narrow walkway that had formed down the middle of the crowd.

O'Brien tugged at Duffy's sleeve. "Quick, now. Let's nip around the side entrance and get in position in the reception room."

Roosevelt stopped inside the Metropole's elegant entry hall and stood with his hands on his hips, surveying the spacious room. Marble columns framed the doorway through which he had entered. Heavy oak panels covered the walls and the windows were dressed with double-thickness velvet draperies done in royal blue and gold. Ahead of him, in front of the reception desk, a row of managers, clerks, housekeepers and bellmen stood in a straight line, as if waiting to be inspected by a visiting general. Roosevelt moved toward them and a thin-faced man stepped forward and bowed to him.

"President Roosevelt, it is indeed an honor to have you stay with us. My name is Potter. I am the manager of the Metropole. The entire staff is at your service." He made a sweeping gesture with his hand to take in the line of people standing behind him."

Roosevelt aimed a beaming smile first at Potter, and then along the line of expectant faces. "It's a pleasure to be here," he boomed, clapping Potter on the shoulder. "But it has been a long journey and I can tell you frankly that I am all in. Could you show us to our quarters?"

"Of course, of course. We've given you the entire east wing on the first floor; top of the staircase and to the right. That's the second floor to you Americans, but here in England we start with the ground floor."

As the manager fawned over Roosevelt, Robert Wallace slipped along the wall, around a huge potted plant, and up the staircase to the next floor. He turned down the corridor as the rest of the entourage began moving up the wide staircase. Wallace paused next to the entrance to Suite 111 at the end of the corridor, distracted by the manager calling to him. Ignoring the manager, Wallace turned the knob and pushed the heavy door open, stepping inside the room.

O'Brien swung the club as Wallace stepped through the doorway, cracking Roosevelt's chief of staff across the back of the head while Duffy slammed the door shut and locked it. Wallace grabbed his head and dropped to the floor, curling into a fetal position.

Duffy kicked Wallace hard in the ribs, and then twice in the kidney before O'Brien stopped him.

"It's not him. It's not Roosevelt."

The two Irishmen looked at the door when the doorknob rattled, and when a pounding began, bolted for the open window. O'Brien was first out, hanging from the narrow ledge and dropping to the ground a dozen feet below. Duffy followed him out and the two ran past surprised onlookers in the still-assembled crowd and disappeared around the corner.

In the corridor outside Suite 111, Potter hammered on the door again, demanding that it be opened.

"Might it not be better if you used a skeleton key to open the door?" Roosevelt asked.

The manager stopped pounding and looked sheepishly at the hardwood floor. "Of course, sir. I should have thought of it."

He produced a small ring of keys from the side pocket of his jacket and fitted a long, narrow key into the lock. Turning it with a swift motion, he pushed the door open and stepped inside.

"Good lord, what has happened here?"

Roosevelt stepped in and pushed the manager aside, kneeling to feel Wallace's pulse. "His pulse is still strong, but you must get a doctor here at once." He stood up and surveyed the room. On the opposite wall, painted in red foot-high capital letters was a message:

LONG LIVE IRELAND

The manager went over to the wall and touched the paint with his fingertip. "It looks like blood."

"I expect that it is supposed to," Roosevelt said. "I also expect that Wallace's assault was meant for me. I cannot imagine why anyone would choose him as a target."

Potter's eyes widened as the import of Roosevelt's comments sunk in. "You still could be in danger."

"I expect that is true too. Perhaps you would consider also calling the local police. We certainly could use them here."

Potter nodded curtly and hustled out of the room, past a throng of onlookers that had gathered there.

"Hang on, Robert," Roosevelt said, stroking Wallace's shoulder. "Help will be here shortly."

❧

Samuel Owst wrinkled his nose and bent closer to the surface of the paper he held in his hand, squinting through pince-nez glasses to make out the sloppy script. Dissatisfied with his progress, he went to the window and held the letter to the light. His eyes widened at what he saw.

"Leaky, get in here." The editor's voice boomed back at him in the tight confines of the office.

When no one appeared at his office door, Owst bellowed again.

Within moments, Leake's face appeared around the edge of the doorframe.

"Come in here and have a look at this," Owst said, thrusting the letter at Leake. "See what you make of it."

Leake tilted the letter to catch the window's light. "Poor penmanship, I should say."

"Never mind that, you dolt. Read the message."

Owst watched Leake's facial muscles stiffen as he read. When he finished, Leake turned to the editor, holding the letter lightly between his thumb and forefinger.

"Are we to believe such a thing?"

"Stranger events have happened, lad."

"But whoever wrote this must be mad."

"Aye, 'tis possible. Let me see that again."

Owst took the ink-stained letter from Leake's hand and re-read the message.

FOR THE GRAPHIC EDITOR:

YOU MUST TELLE YOUR REEDERS NOT TO USE TRAMS. THE COMPANIE TREETS WORKERS UNFAIRELY AND JR EARLE IS THE MAIN CULPRIT. I WILL CONTINU TO HARM RIDERS AND MACHENERY TO MAKE THEM STOP.

ZEUS

Owst dropped the letter onto his desk. "You'll write the story about this for the front page of the next edition. Link it with the derailings, the fires and the assaults on riders."

Leake nodded, his gaze still glued to the letter. "Whoever wrote that note waited a long time to show himself. Why now? And to sign it with the name of a god. That must be the height of egoism."

"Who can tell what goes through such a mind?" Owst sniffed and wrinkled his nose again. "Once you're done with the letter, return it to me. Then I shall pass it along to our police force."

When Leake didn't move, Owst snatched the letter and pushed it against Leake's chest, propelling him backward toward the doorway. "Get on with it, lad. There's no time to waste. We can have the next edition on the streets within a few hours."

After Leake had gone, Owst sank into a chair and rubbed his hands vigorously, thinking of all the papers he would sell.

❧

"Why the bloody hell did you wait so long to deliver the damn thing to me?" Inspector Bradnum, his face flushed and his breathing heavy, stood eye to eye with the *Graphic* editor.

"We needed the time to write the story and get an edition out on the streets," Owst said.

"You must realize this may be a clue of major importance to the case."

Owst glanced away and stepped to the side, but made no reply.

"When did you receive the letter?"

"This morning."

"Was it in the post or delivered by hand."

"It was in the 9 o'clock post."

Bradnum shook his head slowly as if he were following a slowly-moving metronome. "And it took you until the mid-afternoon to bring it to the attention of the police?"

"You will note that the letter is addressed to the editor of the Graphic, which is me," Owst said. "I simply was fulfilling my responsibility to my readers of bringing them the latest news."

Bradnum's tongue worked in his mouth for several moments as if he were rolling a ball bearing around in there. Finally he spoke. "You know damn well your only concern was to sell more newspapers. Did it not occur to you that we might have wanted to keep this letter under wraps in order not to alarm the city's residents?"

"That is not my job. My job is to report the news."

Bradnum stepped in front of the portly editor. "Your civic duty is to cooperate with the police on such matters. If in the future I find you withholding vital evidence in an active investigation, I shall put the manacles on you myself."

Owst recoiled as if he had been struck. "You cannot. You would not."

Bradnum set his mouth in a firm line. "Try me, sir. But I can say that you shall be sorry if you do. Now good day."

The editor bustled out the of office, nearly bumping into Constable Glew as he raised his hand to knock on the doorframe.

"Inspector, you wanted to s-s-see me."

"Aye, Glew. Have a seat." Bradnum waved toward a high-backed chair as he went around his desk. Fishing around in the bottom of a drawer, he withdrew a small canister. He shook out two pills and popped them into his mouth, swallowing quickly. On noticing Glew's stare, he shrugged his shoulders. "Only Brandreth's Pills, my boy. Good for headaches, indigestion and biliousness, all of which test me at the moment."

Glew nodded, but said nothing.

"Have a look at this." Bradnum handed the letter to Glew, who read through it slowly, and then more quickly a second time.

"This is hard to believe, sir. He can't be serious."

"Why do you think it is a 'he'?"

Glew's mouth hung open momentarily before he answered. "A w-w-woman would not do such a thing, would she?"

"I would hope not. But that hope aside, I expect that a woman would not have the strength to grapple with the tram riders who were assaulted in those attacks. In any event, I have an idea that we might pursue and it involves you."

"Me, sir?"

"Aye. I would like you to pose as a tramway worker and see what you might learn by working inside the depot. I have made the necessary arrangements with the depot manager, Gooding. He's the only one who will know your true identity."

"What do you want me to look for?"

"I am convinced that this Zeus is none other than a tramway worker who is in some way disgruntled enough to perpetrate these crimes." Bradnum pointed a finger at Glew. "Mind you, that means this individual is dangerous, so you must be on your guard at all times. Nose around with the other workers and see what you can ferret out."

"How s-s-shall I report to you?"

"You should not be seen coming and going from the police station as it may put you at risk. I can stop at your flat after the end of your shift and we can talk then. On your way now. Report to Mr. Gooding in the morning."

Glew rose and moved toward the door.

"One more thing," Bradnum said, narrowing his eyes to slits. "Be careful over there. You really don't know what you might find."

❧

Robert Wallace sat up gingerly and swung his legs off the bed. He was helped by a white-haired nurse who appeared much more frail than he ever though he could be.

"Thank you nurse. I think I can manage from here."

He stood and swayed momentarily before catching his balance and stepping forward, bracing himself on the doorframe. The elderly nurse scowled at him and tried to again take his elbow, which he pulled from her grasp.

"Again, I thank you for your assistance, but I am capable of walking myself to the door."

"If I had that big gash at the back of me head, I wouldn't be walking nowhere."

Wallace stared at the nurse for a moment, and then smiled widely. "You're right. I should have some help. Would you do so?"

Nodding her head slightly in response, the nurse then guided him down the corridor and to the main entrance of St. Philip's Hospital, where Thomas Taylor, the king's aide, stood.

"My deepest sympathies are with you Mr. Wallace. And those of the king, also." He extended his arm, elbow out, so that Wallace could steady himself on the walk to the touring car drawn up at the covered portico outside. "The king sent me up from London as soon as he received the wire with the news of your injury."

"I am very grateful, but it was not necessary for you to come."

"Nonsense. Of course it was necessary. Your recovery is of our utmost concern. And we also must review the arrangements that have been made for the appearances the king and the president will make together."

Wallace sank back into the soft leather cushions of the touring car and let out a sigh. "That feels wonderful."

Taylor eyed him for a moment. "I shall take you back to the Metropole. I am sure the president will want to see you immediately after we arrive. If you feel up to it after that, perhaps we could sit together for a time and review the arrangements I mentioned."

Wallace sighed again and nodded. Efficient Brits, he thought. Not bothered by a little bump on the head and a kick in the ribs at all, especially if it didn't happen to them.

࿔

The headline in the *Hull Graphic* occupied several inches across the top of the right side of the newspaper.

UNKNOWN PARTY THREATENS TRAM RIDERS WITH HARM

Albert Leake's byline followed on the next line, and then the story began.

> An individual of unknown origin and identity has submitted a letter to the editor of the Graphic, threatening riders on the trams owned by the Hull Tramway Company with physical harm if they continue to ride the trams.
>
> The letter further stated that Mr. J. R. Earle, the managing director of the Hull Tramway Company and owner of Earle Shipbuilding Company here in Hull was the main culprit causing the disturbance. The letter writer promised to harm riders and to cause problems to tramway machinery until Mr. Earle and the officers of the tramway treat workers fairly.
>
> No mention was made of the grievances that may have triggered this unusual action. Mr. Earle was not able to shed any light on the matter at this early stage in the unfolding events.
>
> Hull Inspector Herbert Bradnum is in charge of the investigation concerning the threats and has told the graphic that everything possible is being done to

determine if this is a genuine threat or a colossal hoax.

The full text of the letter to the *Graphic* editor was appended to the end of the story.

の

Bradnum ran his fingers through his thinning hair and puffed out his cheeks in a silent exhalation of air. The previous day's news story in the *Graphic* had generated a continuous stream of unexpected visitors to the Police Station, and especially to his office, all claiming to have information about the unknown Tram Man, as the mysterious threat-maker was now being called. Bradnum had detailed two constables to perform initial interviews in order to fend off the more obvious among those with false tales to tell. But for all their efforts, a steady procession of fakers, prevaricators, egomaniacs and would-be lunatics still found its way into his office.

He leaned forward and planted his hands on his desk, shifting his weight forward toward the turbaned woman sitting in the straight-backed chair. She wore a dress of billowing material so that every time she moved, the fabric floated as if wafted by an unseen breeze. He hair was tucked under a multi-colored scarf that seemed to threaten to slip southward and envelop the woman's forehead entirely and hide her coal-black eyes. Bradnum looked more closely at the smooth unmarked skin of her face and decided she could be anywhere between the ages of thirty and fifty.

"You told the constable outside that you had information about Tram Man, er, about the individual who is making threats to the tram company and its riders."

"That I do." The woman flicked her hand upward as if starting a wave and the fabric of her sleeve floated like a fog settling.

"Perhaps you would care to tell me how you come by the information you are about to give?"

"Indeed. I see the man in my dreams."

Bradnum pushed back from the desk and sighed. "Your dreams. Well, yes, thank you for coming in." He extended his hand toward the door.

The woman didn't move. "You have not heard what I have to tell you yet."

"No, I have not. We need hard evidence in this case, madam. Dreams will not do."

A small smile played across the woman's lips. "You do not know who I am, do you?"

Bradnum shook his head. His hand was still extended toward the door.

"I am Madame Chevellier, the seer of the unknown. It was I who found the Earl of Abernathy's grandson last year when he was taken by ruffians. It was I who directed the industrialist Peter Curzon to the location where his distraught wife had fled. And it was I who shall help you catch the Tram Man." She punctuated her monologue with a curt nod of her head.

Something in the way the woman's eyes shone while she spoke made Bradnum pause before dismissing her out of hand. He certainly could check on her claims of assistance to determine if she had some measure of talent in finding people. But the attestations of pleased clients hardly would be any guarantee of success in the current case, he knew. And, bigod, but what would the superintendent think if he began using the services of a medium to catch criminals? Worse yet, what would the police commissioner say?

Bradnum sat down heavily and looked Madame Chevellier in the eye.

"You intrigue me with your claims of success in other arenas," he began. "But I am wondering how we might make use of your, er, talents, in this case."

If she was upset at his backhanded reference to her past cases, she didn't show it. She extended her hands palms up toward him. "My only goal is to assist the police in stopping this man before he hurts more people. Or worse."

"You say that you see the man in your dreams. Please describe him."

Madame Chevellier closed her eyes and drew a deep breath. "He is a dark shadowy figure in my dreams, yet I feel that he is an intelligent man. In fact, I know he is. Such a plan as he has formed is not the work of a dull mind."

"So you cannot tell me what he looks like."

"Not right now. Perhaps after he visits my dreams again, I will be able to see him better."

"What can you tell me of his plans."

"Only what you already know from his letter."

Bradnum's voice rose. "Then you actually can tell me nothing more than we already know."

Madame Chevellier's eyelids snapped open, and she stared straight at Bradnum. "I make you no promises. I have offered to help and am willing to do so. It takes an enormous amount of energy from me to summon a dream visitor. But I am willing to do this to help you."

Bradnum studied her for a long moment. "All right, then. For the present time, we shall keep our collaboration between ourselves. Do I have your agreement?"

"You do. And once this man is caught because of the help from my dreams, do I have your agreement that you will announce my part in the matter?"

Bradnum had to smile at the woman's impertinence. "By all means. You have my word. But you have work ahead of you, do you not?"

"I shall begin tonight."

When she had gone, Bradnum reached into his bottom drawer and withdrew the canister of Brandreth's pills. Biliousness in his stomach and aching in his head, he thought. Better take three pills for that.

Chapter Eight

The London and North West Railway Special Express thundered along the Liverpool to Manchester rail line, whooshing past quiet villages and sleepy hamlets on its run into the heartland of England. Robert Wallace thought it was especially ironic that the express hurtling across the English countryside was powered by a steam-driven "Atlantic" engine originally designed for use on the Pennsylvania Railroad in 1901. Wallace had scheduled the express to follow the rail line heading practically due east, passing north of Manchester and Huddersfield, and then into the center of the country just south of Leeds where it would pick up the North East Railway line and continue past small towns and through pastureland until arriving at Paragon Station in Hull.

Wallace sat at the far end of a private railcar fitted not with compartments or banks of seats, but with ornate drawing room furniture bolted to the carpet-covered steel floor. Heavy draperies hung at the sides of the windows, held back by elaborate ties to allow the morning sun to stream into the car. On the seat beside him sat a small stack of papers, delivered to him late the previous evening by a king's courier, which he studied with focused intensity. He leaned heavily on the arm of the chair, as his ribs still hurt from the assault in the hotel.

Roosevelt, lounging on a loveseat at the other end of the railcar, watched him closely.

"Well, Robert, are you going to tell me what's in those papers you have your nose buried in or am I to be kept in the dark until it all happens?" He was smiling and his eyes glinted behind his eyeglasses.

"Yes, sir. I was simply reviewing the arrangements to be sure that nothing was omitted."

"Omitted?" Roosevelt guffawed and stood up, his hands on his hips. "The only thing that concerns me is how many pheasant there are at this place — what's it called — Elmsdale House."

"Elmfield House, sir. The correct name is Elmfield House."

"Well, bully," Roosevelt said, still smiling. "Do you think it possible to shoot a hundred pheasant, Robert?"

"I'm sure if it can be done, you will be the one to reach that mark, sir."

Roosevelt cocked his head at the thought. "You are a sly one, Robert. Sly, indeed."

Wallace nodded, and then began a recitation of the arrangements that the king's staff had made for the president's arrival at Paragon Station that afternoon and his transfer to the Grosvenor Hotel. He moved on through the reception and dinner to be given in Roosevelt's honor by the king, finishing with a description of the short trip to Elmfield House that they would make the next day.

"Ah, now we get to the good part. You know Robert, I really should check my Parker again. Is it in the next car?"

"It is, Mr. President, but perhaps it might be wiser to allow the Parker to rest easy until we get to Elmfield House. After all, you shouldn't need it between here and there."

Roosevelt clucked his tongue. "You are absolutely right. But my blood is up for some sport and it's two days away. I certainly am looking forward to this match-up with the king."

"I know you are, sir. But remember, the king is a crack shot himself. You should be on your toes and shoot straight."

Roosevelt grinned widely at Wallace, the sunlight gleaming off his white teeth. "It is the only way I ever shoot, Robert. The only way."

❧

Inspector Bradnum stepped off the tram and onto the pavement at Queen Victoria Square in front of the grand edifice of City Hall. Taking the steps two at a time, he brushed through the entryway and mounted the staircase to the first floor where the mayor's office was located. Inside, a pinched-faced woman offered him a seat in a room dominated by a long table surrounded by high-backed chairs. After he had cooled his heels for five minutes, a door in the side wall of the room opened and the mayor stepped in, followed by a file of men in dark suits and waistcoats. The council members, Bradnum guessed. Last through the door was J. R. Earle. They all found seats around the long table, leaving Bradnum alone at the far end.

"You are here to tell us what the police have done to protect us," Earle began. "Get on with it."

Bradnum bit back a sharp reply and folded his hands in front of him. He drew a deep breath and started talking. He laid out the protective measures he and the superintendent had agreed on for the council members. For the mayor, he said, they had decided on added protection in the form of a bodyguard because of the high visibility of the office. He looked Earle dead in the eyes when he said the same precautions as those for the mayor would be extended to him.

"Don't need the damn protection. I can well take care of myself," Earle said.

"J. R., you should not be hasty," the mayor began, but was cut off by a black look from Earle.

"I said I don't need the protection and shall not have it around me. Is that understood?" He glared directly at Bradnum.

Bradnum held Earle's gaze for several moments before responding. "If you choose to refuse police protection, then there is nothing else we can offer you, Mr. Earle."

Earle looked away first. "Then that is the way it shall be. Use the constables elsewhere. I shall not need them." Earle rose, and without acknowledging any of the others, stomped out of the room.

The mayor looked as if he had swallowed a bitter potion. "Mr. Earle sometimes gets his blood up. Perhaps he will reconsider at a later time."

Bradnum forced a tight smile. "The Hull police shall be pleased to oblige whenever we are needed."

Constable James Glew glanced to the left and right as he moved through the wide doors of the rear entrance of the Tramway Depot, the entryway most of the employees used. He hoped that no one would notice him or challenge his right to be there, although Inspector Bradnum had assured him that the manager had fabricated a plausible story to cover his presence in the depot. The constable closed his eyes for a moment and said a mental prayer the Inspector was right. Glew wasn't by nature a religious man, but when confronted with unknown and unseen dangers, he usually turned toward a generic almighty being who might assist him in his plight.

He found the corridor to Gooding's office and presented himself to the stern-faced woman who sat behind the desk in front of the depot manager's door.

"James Glew," he said, shifting from foot to foot. "Mr. Gooding said to report to him this morning."

The woman held up a finger toward him as if to test the wind direction and then disappeared into the back office without knocking. She returned within a half-minute.

"He says to go right in."

Glew stepped into the tightly-stuffed office and immediately bumped against a stack of books resting alongside a chair covered with more papers. He successfully grabbed the books before they could sprawl across the floor and backed slowly away from them.

"Constable, I will not keep ye long."

Glew's eyes widened. "D-d-d-don't call me that in here. I'm only one of the workers, remember."

Gooding blushed, but ignored the rebuke. "I have assigned ye to the electrical generation department," he said. "Back there ye will not have to deal with the trams and will be supervised by an experienced engineer. His name is Purling." He jerked his thumb behind him, toward the rear of the tram yard where Glew had entered. "Go see him now and get started."

The manager picked up a sheaf of papers from his desk and bent his head close to them. Glew, finding himself staring at the top of the man's head, began to respond, but changed his mind and held his tongue.

Outside in the yard, he eyed the looming presence of the electrical generation shed. The place had a pulse of its own, he thought, made palpable by the hum of the generators and the coursing electricity that flowed from it to power the trams.

"Do you require some help?" The man stood at the corner of the shed, shielding his eyes as he watched Glew.

"N-n-no. I'm newly assigned here."

The man stepped up and thrust out his hand. "William Cole. I'm a tram driver. Had to bring number 56 back because of a bad spring. She's listing quite badly."

Glew had his hand on the latch to the shed's door, but made no move to open it. Instead, he shook hands with Cole. "D-d-do you know anything about Mr. Purling? I'm to work with him."

Cole barked out a laugh. "You'll find him odd at first. But remember that he has forgotten more about motors and electrical generation than most of us will ever know. Pay him close attention."

"Thanks for the advice."

"Good luck. I'll see you around the depot." Cole waved and headed back around the side of the shed.

Glew, his hand shaking lightly, cracked open the door and stepped inside, letting his eyes adjust to the dimmer light.

"Who the devil are you?" The man who challenged him sat astride a low stool and held a mass of twisted wiring in his hands. He had a darkish complexion and a shock of hair that seemed to try to fly in all directions. He was not smiling.

"James Glew. I w-w-was assigned here by Mr. Gooding just now."

"That dolt. Now that you have finished with him, you shall be better off. The man knows nothing about how these trams are cared for."

"I was told to find a man named Purling. Is that y-y-you?"

The man on the stool studied him for a few seconds. "It is me." He cracked the semblance of a small smile. "So you are to be my assistant." Purling shook his head as he looked Glew up and down. "I never thought the old buggar would actually listen to me and get me some help."

He pushed himself off the stool and dropped the wiring onto the stone-flagged floor. "Come along. I will show you the operation of the place. But be wary," he said, stopping and holding up his hand as if to stop Glew. "This is a dangerous place with voltages that can fry a man quicker than a chicken on a hot fire. You best listen to what I have to tell you."

Glew nodded. "I'm all ears."

"Capital. Then pay attention. We begin over here," Purling said, walking toward the closest generating unit.

Glew followed, wondering how much electrical generation knowledge he would actually have to learn.

Patrick Sweeney tugged at the bill of his cap and pulled it low on his forehead, forcing his longish brown hair over his ears. He looked east along Carr Lane toward City Hall, and then back across the road to the Grosvenor Hotel. The morning sunlight threw sharply-slanted shadows across the hotel's lower floors, while its upper stories were bathed in bright contrast to the dimness below. A flurry of activity at the pavement in front of the Grosvenor's main entry caught his eye, but he lost sight of the arriving motorcars and their disembarking passengers as a tram passed in front of him, westbound on Carr Lane. When the tram had gone, Sweeney studied the four top-hatted gentlemen posing at the base of the steps, and after a long inspection decided they were not the individuals who he had to be concerned about.

He drew back deeper into the recessed doorway of the Speckled Hen Public House and leaned against the weathered doorpost. He had been watching the arriving guests at the hotel for the better part of the morning and had nothing to show for his surveillance efforts except sore feet and an aching back from standing on the unyielding stone walkway. The details Gallagher had gotten from Murphy, the king's clerk, must have been wrong, he thought. Either that, or the arrangements for the transport from Liverpool to Hull had been changed after Murphy was privy to them. If that were the case, it would explain why Roosevelt still had not showed up at the hotel.

Sweeney rubbed the back of his neck and dug his thick fingertips into the cords at the base of his neck, trying to relieve the ache there. He could have done his surveillance at Paragon Station where the president's train would arrive, but he had detailed that task to Gallagher. Sweeney wanted to be sure that Roosevelt transferred to the hotel. He wanted to see him step inside the Grosvenor. He didn't want to assume that the man had gone there. If he had taken up post at the station, Sweeney could never have been sure. This way, he thought, I'll have him in my sights.

He smiled thinly and tugged on his cap again, thinking of what still had to be done.

☙

A mile west of the small passenger station at Goole on the North East Railway line, a flashing red railway signal at the entrance of a cutting directed the engineer of the president's express train into a siding that looped around the cut and lay between a marsh on the north and fields dotted with gnarled trees and shrubs, and a handful of ancient cottages on the south. The engineer pulled the brake and the big Atlantic engine hissed to a halt, releasing billows of steam onto each side of the track.

As the train shuddered to a stop, conductor J. H. Heron checked his pocket watch. Something's amiss, he thought. Expresses aren't shunted into sidings. Something must be wrong on the main track. Out on the rear car's platform, he swung down to the ground and began to make his way along the side of the railbed toward to engine, its boiler still spewing steam. Apparently the engineer didn't plan to be here long, he thought, because he's keeping up a full head of steam.

Behind the big Atlantic engine and its coal tender rode two mail coaches containing luggage and the personal effects of the president and his entourage, followed by three first class carriages, the center one of which housed the president and his assistant. As Heron strode alongside the president's coach, the sole of his boot slipped on a flat, angled rock and he dropped onto all fours, catching himself from sliding off the roadbed and into the nearby ditch. As he began to straighten up, his eyes widened at what he saw inside the rails under the president's coach. Heron edged closer and involuntarily held his breath as he put his head under the coach and examined the three piles of dynamite, each taped into a pyramid about a foot high. The three pyramids were wired together by a length of fuse that disappeared under the rail closest to him.

Heron ran his thumb along the outside base of the rail and loosened the gravel there. The fuse continued under the gravel and down the roadbed into the ditch.

Leaping to his feet, Heron ran the length of the train, shouting for the engineer to release the brake.

Shamus Loughrey lay in the tall grass at the edge of the pasture, overlooking the railway siding. He was masked from view by scrub brush and uneven piles of stones that had long ago been turned out of the field to form a rough wall along its edge. Loughrey had protested that he should not be used as the sharp point of the spear, so to speak. He had told Gallagher that his talent lay in ferreting out information and compromising people in sensitive positions. Gallagher had simply laughed and ordered him to travel from London to

Goole to take on this nasty bit of business. He said it would be good for Loughrey to experience the practical side of an operation, even if it meant being inconvenienced.

Loughrey sighed and rolled back onto his stomach. Then he heard the train whistle. He raised up enough to see over the grass in time to watch the special express steam into the siding and stop exactly where Gallagher had said it would. The second car from the end, the president's car, was directly over the explosives. As the big engine hissed steam, Loughrey struck a match and touched it to the end of the fuse on the ground in front of him. The fuse sparked, and then hissed and sputtered to life, quickly burning through the grass toward the ditch and the rail line beyond.

As he turned to leave, Loughrey saw a conductor jump to the ground from the rear carriage. No matter, Loughrey thought, you're much too late.

ȗ

As Heron clambered up the side steps into the engine, the engineer put his hand out to stop him.

"What the bloody hell do you think you're playing at?"

"Move the train. Get the train moving."

"There's a bloody red signal in front of me. I cannot." The engineer stood with his arms crossed and his feet planted wide apart.

Heron took a deep breath to steady his breathing. "You must move the train now. There's dynamite on the track and the president's car is sitting directly over it."

The engineer's face drained to white. Then he spun toward the controls and yanked on a long black handle, pushing it back against the boiler housing. With the brake off, he grabbed the throttle and pulled it open too much, causing the big Atlantic's wheels to spin on the steel rails.

"Easy, man. Easy. Get her rolling."

Sweat had appeared on the engineer's brow. "Aye. Give me a second."

"I don't know that we have a second."

The engineer eased the throttle back toward the housing until the engine's wheels slowed enough to get a bite on the rails. The Atlantic began to inch forward, and with the application of more throttle from the engineer, started to pick up speed, emerging from the siding and onto the main track. As the luggage coaches crossed onto the main line, the fuse burned out of the ditch and up to the edge of the railbed. As the president's car swung onto the main line, the dynamite exploded, sending a concussive shock wave crashing against the last carriage, shredding its door and blackening the exterior. But it remained on the track and within five minutes, the express shuddered to a stop at Goole Station in Hull.

Chapter Nine

Madame Chevellier glared at the beefy constable behind the high counter and pressed up on her tiptoes.

"You simply do not understand. It is a matter of the greatest urgency that I speak with Inspector Bradnum immediately."

The constable fixed her with a fish-eyed stare and pointed to a bench against the wall. "As I told you earlier, you must wait."

"But you have not even summoned him yet."

The constable looked at her as if she had made a joke. "For a gypsy? I hardly think it necessary."

She was on the verge of a tart reply when she heard Inspector Bradnum's voice coming from the back of the large room. "Inspector. Inspector Bradnum. I must speak with you." She waved her arms as if signaling someone in semaphore.

"Eh, who is that? Oh, Madame Chevellier," Bradnum said, striding over to the counter.

"You know this woman?"

"Indeed, Constable. I believe she has information for me at this very moment, is that not correct, Madame?"

"I do, I do," she said, swishing around the side of the counter while throwing the constable a black look. "Inspector, terrible things are about to happen..."

Bradnum pressed his forefinger to his lips. "In my office, please."

She sat in the straight backed chair, edging forward so that she was balanced on the edge of the seat.

"You have information for me about Tram Man?"

She sighed heavily. "It is much more serious than that. It concerns the American president."

"Roosevelt?"

She nodded, keeping her gaze riveted on Bradnum. "I saw him last night clearly in my dream. He was dressed in a shooting outfit and carried a shotgun through a field. Several shooting partners were to the left and right of him, but he was leading the way." She stopped and breathed deeply, twisting her hands together in her lap.

"And then?"

"What I saw next was not entirely clear. As the president reached a low wall shielded by bushes and some trees, a shot sounded and he clutched his chest. Then he collapsed."

Bradnum stood at the side of his desk, looking down at her.

"Collapsed? As if he had been shot?"

"Exactly as if he were shot."

"Did you see who shot him?"

Madame Chevellier looked down at her feet and shook her head. "That was the unclear part. I could see the flash of the shot from the shadow of the trees, but not the person who made the shot."

Bradnum dropped into his chair and pulled his hand across his mouth. "It's unbelievable."

She looked up at him sharply. "I am telling you the truth of what I saw in the dream. I had prepared myself to receive the dreams that night and this is what came to me. You can believe it or not. But if it happens as I say it will, you shall be sorry you did not heed me."

"Madame Chevellier, you must remember that we spoke of using your dreams to help with the Tram Man case. Now you come to me with this tale of a possible attempt on the American president's life. It is a bit beyond belief."

She stood and brushed her full skirt flat against her thighs. Looking him straight in the eye, she said, "His blood will be on your hands, Inspector. You should consider that before you dismiss what I've told you."

Then she left the office, leaving Bradnum with a puzzled look on his face.

಄

Inspector Bradnum stared at the doorway and wondered how much faith he should put in the psychic's claims. He had checked on her and determined she actually had some successes in locating missing people through her dreams. Or at least that was how she claimed she did it. But this business with the American president. He would look a right fool if he went to the superintendent and said he wanted to warn the president of a possible attack on his life, based on the dreams of a gypsy woman. Bradnum reached into the bottom drawer and withdrew the canister of Brandreth's pills. He swallowed two of them. Tonight would be the time to allow the opium smoke to work it's magic on me, he thought. The Brandreth's pills would have to hold him until then. In the meantime, he still had to work on the Tram Man case. He flipped open his notebook and looked at the next name on his list to interview. Richard Purling.

A half-hour later he entered the electric generating shed at the Tramway Depot. As he rounded the back of a large motor humming with electricity, he came face to face with Constable Glew. Bradnum quickly held up his hand.

"Can you tell me where I might find the mechanic, Richard Purling?"

Glew's eyes were wide, but he had enough sense to play along. "Just over there," he said, pointing to a workbench at the back of the cavernous room. "The man working on the wiring."

"Thank you." Bradnum touched the brim of his hat and moved toward the workbench.

"Richard Purling?"

"And who wants to know? I am busy."

"Inspector Herbert Bradnum of the Hull Police." Bradnum showed his warrant card.

For a fleeting moment Bradnum saw fear on Purling's face, but it was quickly replaced with a snarl.

"What, no crimes for you to solve? Must you be pestering law-abiding citizens?"

"We have been told that you have grievances with the tramway company. Perhaps you would like to elaborate on them for me?"

Purling stared at him for a long moment. "Aye, I have grievances. But they are nothing I will speak to you about." He spat on the floor at Bradnum's feet.

Bradnum looked down at the spittle, and then back at Purling. "A word to the wise, Mr. Purling. Don't get too full of yourself with the police. It can have nasty consequences. Good day."

அ

The Special Express steamed into Paragon Station and came to a halt at the main platform as a brass band struck up the American national anthem. A huge crowd of well-wishers and gawkers had turned out to see Roosevelt arrive and had crammed every square foot of the platform, cheering and calling out his name. As the president stepped from his carriage and raised his arms in greeting, the crowd bellowed louder and surged forward, enveloping the dozen policemen who had formed a security line between them and the carriage.

Roosevelt was quickly surrounded by a hoard of Britons, many applauding him, some clapping him on the shoulders, all while the police tried to fend off as many individuals in the crowd as they could. Roosevelt began walking down the platform and as he did the crowd parted in front of him as if her were Moses opening up the Red Sea. He could hear snatches of shouts cast in his direction.

"Bully for you."

"Welcome to Hull."

"Teddy, you're our man."

Roosevelt exited the platform behind a wedge of five policemen who led him and Wallace out of the station and into the rear of a waiting automobile. But the crowd was not to be dissuaded and surrounded the big Napier saloon car, which had its top down, still cheering and applauding. Seeing no other way, Roosevelt stood up on the rear seat and raised his arms for quiet.

"My new friends," he began, smiling widely, "it is indeed a pleasure to be greeted by such a warm welcome as you have given me today."

The crowd began cheering again, and Roosevelt again quieted them.

"I am most interested in meeting your King Edward and spending some time taking in the sights of your lovely city. And we shall see more of each other when the king and I attend the celebration of your tramway's electrification later in the week."

The crowd erupted again and Roosevelt sat down, smiling and waving. It took some minutes, but finally the policemen cleared a path through the throng and the saloon car turned out the station approach on onto Brook Street, heading toward the Grosvenor Hotel on Carr Lane.

❧

"What do you mean someone tried to blow up Roosevelt's train?"

Bradnum could scarcely believe his ears. First the psychic telling him about her dreams of the president being shot and now this. He snatched the telegram flimsy sheet from the constable and read through it quickly. "By Jove, it is true. Fortunately, no one was injured." He looked at the flimsy again. "Some damage to the last carriage in the train, but nothing that cannot be put right."

He looked at the constable. "Do we know where the president's train is now?"

"I have just had some of the constables assigned to Paragon return, sir. The president's train has arrived and he has disembarked. He is on the way to the Grosvenor Hotel. He should be there by now."

Bradnum folded the telegram into quarters and stuffed it into his breast pocket.

"I will be with the chief constable. After that, you can find me at the Grosvenor Hotel."

❧

Patrick Sweeney had to move his watching place when the Speckled Hen opened for the day and he settled for a narrow alley between the public house and a tailor shop. As he shifted his weight against the building to ease his aching legs, a black Napier saloon car drew up in front of the Grosvenor with four top hatted men in the back. Sweeney edged forward for a better view. Clearly, the man with the unframed eyeglasses perched on the bridge of his nose and the wide smile was Roosevelt.

Sweeney watched as the foursome exited the car and then climbed the steps into the entry hall of the Grosvenor. Splendid, Sweeney thought. He crossed the street and made his way along a narrow lane to the west of the hotel that led to a delivery area at the rear. A small lorry with its rear doors wide open was backed up to a doorway. Sweeney looked inside the lorry. Empty. There was no one in the rear yard, so he ducked through the doorway and disappeared into a storeroom at the back of the hotel.

Chapter Ten

"The president is indisposed and not available. Not even for the police." Robert Wallace stood with his feet wide apart and his arms crossed. He wasn't smiling.

Inspector Bradnum pointed to a floral-patterned sofa in the sitting room on the second floor of the Grosvenor Hotel. "May we sit and discuss the problem?"

Wallace nodded and sat down stiffly in a leather chair opposite Bradnum.

"Mr. Wallace, I trust you have recovered sufficiently from the unfortunate incident in Liverpool." Wallace inclined his head in acknowledgment and Bradnum continued. "The superintendent has asked me to convey his regrets that he is unable to be here personally to arrange for the special protection of the president. Nonetheless, I think you will find that we are quite capable of putting together a plan that will meet the president's needs."

"What sort of plan did you have in mind?"

Bradnum leaned forward and planted his elbows on his knees, steepling his hands under his fleshy chin as if in prayer. "I daresay we shall pull out all the stops, as you Americans say. We already have detailed a squad of a half-dozen policemen in civilian clothes to patrol the interior of the

Grosvenor night and day while the president is in residence. Constables in uniform are stationed at the major entrances to the hotel and will closely monitor the comings and goings of individuals at their respective locations."

Bradnum drew a deep breath and continued. "Just down the street is the Hull City Hall. We have commandeered several rooms there to serve as a police command post while the president is here. Its close location will allow for a speedy relief of our men on duty at the Grosvenor. When the president moves about in the town, if he is so inclined to do so, we will assign two constables to be with him at all times. Each will be armed with a Webley revolver."

Wallace's eyebrows raised. "It was my impression that British policemen did not carry firearms. Only those sticks — what do you call them?"

"Truncheons." Bradnum sat back and let the sofa's cushions envelop him. "These are unusual times, Mr. Wallace, and such times call for extraordinary measures. We shall do all in our power to ensure that the president has a safe and memorable visit here in Hull. The security precautions I have outlined will be repeated at Elmfield House, with some minor modifications because of its location, during the time the king is in residence and when the president transfers there."

Wallace stood and a small smile crept across his face. He extended his hand to Bradnum. "Thank you for your concern over my health, Inspector. And for your thorough preparations on behalf of the president. It all seems in order."

Bradnum grasped Wallace' hand in a firm grip. "I assume you shall be the point of contact for any issues involving the president?"

"That is correct. But we should strive for few or no issues, if you get my meaning."

"I do. And I mean no disrespect, but nothing would make me happier than not to have to speak to you about this again." Bradnum clapped his hat on his head and headed for the hotel lobby.

Indeed, he thought, I should be glad to be done with the entire job.

&

King Edward VII, lounging against the side wall of his traveling carriage as the Royal Express slowed, watched the looming bulk of the Argyle Street bridge pass overhead at the West Parade Junction, where the London and Northeast Railway lines made a quadruple-X cross just east of Hull's Paragon Station. The carriage wheels screeched as the train passed a row of terrace houses, their sides and rears sooty from the coal dust blast of thousands of engines that had traveled the route before. The Londesborough Barracks stretched away to the north and the king could see a squad of men lined up at the entrance to the Miniature Rifle Range. He pointed toward the shooters.

"Thomas, there is an example of our fine fellows under arms exercising their skills."

Thomas Taylor leaned closer to the window for a better view. "Yes, your majesty. Don't they look splendid?"

The king looked at Taylor and raised his eyebrows. "Let's hope they can shoot those .22 rifles as well as I can my double. We need soldiers in the ranks, not popinjays." The king emphasized the word "soldiers."

The shadow of the Park Street bridge dimmed the interior of the carriage for a moment, and the train slowed even more, finally edging to a stop at platform ten on the far northern end of the station.

Out on the platform, a dozen porters stood in a line along the edge of the concrete deck, waiting for the word to begin unloading the carriage stuffed with the belongings of the king and his entourage. Within minutes the king emerged from his carriage and the row of porters bowed as if someone had pulled a string controlling them. The king smiled and waved at them, and led by Taylor and two constables, made his way through the iron gateway at the end of the platform before disappearing out one of the station's north doorways.

Drawn up outside on Collier 's Street were two Napier saloon cars, each with its engine running and its driver ready. The king pulled himself into the rear of the first vehicle, as did Taylor, while the constables and two assistants took the second car. Fifteen minutes later, after following a circuitous route through Hull, the vehicles pulled into the graveled drive at Elmfield House and parked opposite a fountain where water gushed from the outstretched hands of the statue of a goddess.

"Attractive sculpture," the Taylor said, pointing to the fountain. "I wonder who it represents."

"Actually it is the Roman goddess Minerva," the king replied. "J. R. Earle had it commissioned because he and Minerva share the same birthday, March twentieth." The king shot Taylor a mischievous look. "Or so I am told."

A constable opened the door to the entrance hall of the house and standing in the doorway was J. R. Earle, feet splayed wide and his hands on his hips.

"Your majesty, I was about to give up on you and take a stroll out on the estate alone to scare up some pheasant. But now that you have arrived, we can do so together."

The king chuckled and put a beefy hand on Earle's shoulder. "You know there's damned little that will keep me from a shooting holiday."

"Well we shall certainly fulfill your wishes when it comes to the shooting. My keepers tell me the fields are loaded with game — pheasant, rabbit, even deer. You shall have your choice."

The king winked and smiled thinly. "I am looking forward to the pheasant shoot with Roosevelt. Immensely."

"Then perhaps we should get out there and view the field to re-familiarize you with Elmfield. Will that do?"

"Splendid idea, Earle. Simply splendid," the king said and clapped him on the shoulder again. "I like the sound of that."

Albert Leake leaned back and the old pine chair creaked ominously, its structural members protesting at the stressing movement. He held the proof at arm's length to ease the strain his eyes had developed in the past year. Elderly eye, a colleague had called it. The farsightedness that came with aging apparently had caught up with him earlier than he had though possible, likely because of the laborious proofreading he had to do. Leake dropped the page to desktop and stretched his neck up and back, listening to the crackling and popping of the tendons releasing their tension. Picking up the paper again, he began to reread the story.

KING & PRESIDENT TO CELEBRATE TRAMWAY ELECTRIFICATION

By Albert Leake

A special event is in the making at the weekend as King Edward VII and American President Theodore Roosevelt will help the Hull Tramway Company celebrate ten years of electrification of its lines with a ceremony at the tramway depot on Manchester Street off the Hessle Road.

The King, who is entertaining the American president before Roosevelt makes his way to Africa for a safari, is residing at Elmfield House with J.R. Earle, the owner of Earle's Shipbuilding & Engineering Yard and a director of the Hull Tramway Company.

Roosevelt is currently lodged at the Grosvenor Hotel, but is expected to join the king and Earle at Elmfield House for a taste of English country house living and a spot of pheasant shooting on the estate.

Leake dropped the paper to the desktop again and rubbed his eyes. He had re-read the story several times and it all appeared fine. The balance of the article gave more details about the tramway ceremony and the planned activities at Elmfield House. He had seen the information so many times, the words now tended to blur together.

Abruptly, Leake rose from behind the desk and pushed the paper aside. He was through for now; the story was fine. It was time to find a bit of supper and a pint. He paused at the main doorway to the *Graphic* office and cast a long glance back at his desk. Turning quickly, he went through the door and headed down the street.

❧

Teddy Roosevelt set the coffee cup gently on its saucer and turned to Wallace. "Well, Robert, what is all this nonsense about protection from the local police?"

"Mr. President, the police are very concerned about the explosion on the rail line. They are convinced it's the work of

Irish terrorists, intent on involving you in their political difficulties with the English."

"Is that what this is all about? Haven't you told them that I am the man who led the Rough Riders up San Juan Hill? I don't need special protection."

"Begging your pardon, sir, but these events are exceptional. First we had the problem at the Metropole Hotel in Liverpool. It's difficult to ignore a message of 'Long Live Ireland' scrawled on a hotel room wall in red paint. Especially when the warning is accompanied by a brutal beating." Wallace massaged his ribs as he talked.

Roosevelt softened the look on his face. "I am thoroughly mortified that you have suffered on my behalf, Robert."

"I have no intent on seeking your sympathy, Mr. President." Wallace stood and began pacing in front of the windows. "I am simply concerned about your safety. The episode on the train where we were shunted onto a siding and nearly blown up has made the threats very real. Mr. President, you could be in extreme danger here in England. I think that we might consider canceling the rest of your appearances and leaving straight for Africa at the earliest possible sailing date."

Roosevelt stared at Wallace for so long that his chief assistant was forced to look away.

"I will not run from any man or group of men," Roosevelt said, rising from his chair. "We shall proceed as we have planned with the itinerary here. We shall enjoy the Grosvenor's hospitality and that of Elmfield House in the next few days. I'll shoot with the king and Earle. And I shall damn well win the wager for the case of Dom Perignon." Roosevelt pointed at Wallace. "See to it that everything goes as we have planned. I shall not miss a thing. No Irish thugs will push Teddy Roosevelt around."

Roosevelt turned and went to the window, staring out toward the River Ouse.

❧

Richard Purling slipped along the side of the huge electric generating motor and ran his hand along its cold steel flank. Those devilish capitalists, he thought. Their only concern was for their own well-being and gratification through profits. No concern for the working man, he harrumphed. No sir. J. R. Earle and his board of directors only were occupied by how much money they could wring out of the populace of the city. Purling stopped in mid-stride and stroked the motor again. They had no appreciation for the complexity of the machinery that provided them their profits, he thought. And because of their thoughtlessness, he would be sure they would become aware.

Purling stopped at the workbench in the rear of the cavernous room and chose a selection of hand tools — two wrenches, a pair of pliers and a slotted screwdriver. At the control panel to the number two motor, he removed the covering plate and reached inside, being careful not to allow his flesh to touch the electrical contacts that bristled on the inside of the panel. Within ten minutes, he had rerouted the main electrical lines to a switch he had mounted at the back of the bottom of the cabinet. If anyone looked inside the control panel, everything would seem normal unless the wiring were moved to expose his switch.

Purling stood back and admired his handiwork, and then reached forward and put his thumb and forefinger around the toggle switch. He put pressure on the metal switch and felt it move slightly in its housing. At the movement, he released the pressure and allowed the switch to return to its neutral position.

No sense in alarming the populace with a spectacular discharge of electricity right now, he thought. Just wait until the ceremony on the weekend. Then, he would show them.

&

Constable Glew shrank back into the shadows beside a pile of wooden crates alongside the east wall of the electric generating shed. He watched Purling come into the shed and walk directly to the workbench, where he collected a handful of tools. Glew peered around the edge of a crate and watched as Purling busied himself inside the control panel of the number two electric generating motor. Once Purling had finished his business, he shut the cabinet, returned the tools to the bench, and left the building.

Glew waited several minutes to be sure he was alone and that Purling would not return. He crossed to the control panel and pulled open the cover, staring at the mass of wiring and switches inside. Purling had instructed him on the basics of wiring and electrical design, but the colored tentacles that snaked out in all directions inside the control panel made Glew's head hurt. He reached out as if to touch one of the switches, but pulled his hand back as if it had been burnt by a hot stove.

This was a conundrum for someone else to solve, he thought, shutting the control panel door. I'll let Inspector Bradnum puzzle it out.

He shut the panel door and was about to leave the building when the door creaked open and William Cole stood in the doorway.

"Glew, how are you? Is the work to your liking?"

"It is good enough. You were right about Mr. Purling."

Cole laughed and put a hand on Glew's shoulder. "Come along with me. I'll stand you to a pint down at the Fox and Hounds."

Inside the public house, the pair perched on low stools near the stone fireplace. Cole raised his pint in a mock toast.

"To learning the finer elements of electricity."

Glew drank deeply and set the glass down gingerly. "Why do you think Mr. Purling is so secretive?"

"Secretive, is he? Damn eccentric, if you ask me."

"What I mean is that he tells me things about the work as if he doesn't want anyone else to overhear. It's like he's telling me secrets."

"Maybe they are." Cole took another swallow of his ale. "What has he been showing you?"

Glew told him. He recounted his day from the morning to the late afternoon, when Purling had left. When Glew finished his tale, Cole's forehead was creased with horizontal furrows. When their glasses were empty, the two men shook hands again and parted company, but Glew could see that Cole had something on his mind.

Chapter Eleven

The king cleared his throat as he entered the ornate dining room, attracting the attention of everyone present except J. R. Earle, who had his face buried so far into the *Hull Graphic* that his nose practically touched the page. As the king rounded the far end of the elongated oak table, Earle looked up, seemingly startled.

"Eddy! I didn't hear you come in. Sit down, sit down."

The king eased into a chair at the side of table's corner. He fixed Earle with a steely stare. "I have asked you in the past not to address me in that way, J. R. You take too many liberties simply because we grew up together." He picked up the linen napkin and snapped it out fully, and then dropped it onto his lap.

Earle seemed as if he were about to reply, but said nothing.

After the staff wheeled in two carts laden with silver serving dishes, served the two men, and then disappeared back into the pantry, the king cocked his head toward Earle.

"I suppose sooner or later you shall tell me about the arrangements for the shooting party."

Earle looked as if he had been surprised stealing an apple from a greengrocer's cart.

"Of course, sire, of course. The usual suspects shall be here with us. There's Lord Carrington who you know to be a keen sportsman. Then there is the Duke of Cumberland, Lord Roseberry, MP Campbell and a few others."

He paused and surveyed the room as if he were searching for a spy behind the draperies. Earle continued in a near-conspiratorial whisper.

"President Roosevelt will be joining us shortly. I propose that he and I shoot together so that we might have a friendly wager between ourselves. Actually, you may want to get in on the wager too. After all, there is no reason why you should not profit from my success."

"You assume that my wager would be on you to shoot more pheasant than Roosevelt does."

Earle drew back from the table like he had been slapped. "You believe that he will shoot better than me?"

The king dabbed at the corner of his mouth with his napkin. "I have heard Roosevelt is a keen shot and rarely misses his target. It is said of him both on the shooting field and in politics too."

"He shall not bag more pheasant than I do. You mark me."

The king smiled widely. "Perhaps the two of us should wager on it. My wager with Roosevelt is a case of Dom Perignon. Ours shall be the same. Agreed?"

Earle barely nodded before excusing himself and leaving the dining room.

❧

The storeroom at the back of the Grosvenor Hotel was crowded with crates, barrels and shelving heaped with the kinds of supplies necessary to keep a first class hotel running smoothly. Floor to ceiling bins lined the wall across from Patrick Sweeney, most of them filled to bursting with dry goods, soap, towels, bed linens and hotel livery clothing. Sweeney moved to the center of the room and struck a pose, standing straight and folding his hands behind him at the small of his back. He thrust his chest out as he took a deep breath and angled his head downward to get a better look at his image in the hand mirror propped up in the corner of a bin. Amazing, he thought. If I didn't know differently, I'd think me a member of the bleedin' hotel staff. He adjusted his collar one last time, and after hiding the mirror at the bottom of the bin, strode out into the service corridor.

He found a set of stairs at the end of the corridor, leading both toward the cellars below and the first floor above. Mounting the stairs with a quiet tread, he listened the whole time for sounds of anyone approaching, but heard nothing until he reached the first floor level and cracked open the staircase doorway. A gaggle of women in wildly-elaborate hats eased past him, talking loudly and making excited gestures.

"He is such an imposing figure. I thought I might faint."

"Griselda, take a hold on yourself. He may be a striking figure, but he is still a man."

"And what a man he must be. And to be president of the United States. He must be the most powerful man in the world, after the king."

"I heard the staff talking in the entry hall. One of them said that Roosevelt and his entourage have taken up an entire wing on the second floor. The north wing."

"We shall likely never get a glimpse of him again."

Sweeney backed through the still-open doorway and closed the door noiselessly. Taking the stairs two at a time, he arrived at the second floor slightly breathless. This is no time to lose your wits, Boyo, he told himself. Slow down. After taking a couple of deep breaths, he stepped into the second floor corridor and paced along the thick carpet toward the north wing.

❧

Inspector Bradnum knocked again on the massive door to Elmfield House and was startled when the door was opened just after he finished pounding on it.

"Ah, Inspector. Please do come in."

The housekeeper led him to a sitting room off the entrance hall where he amused himself by estimating the original size of the mounted animals that adorned the walls. A few minutes later the door burst open and J. R. Earle strode into the room.

"Inspector, if you insist on continuing to show up at my home, I may have to lay in special accommodations for you."

Earle stood ramrod straight with his hands at his side. Bradnum could not detect even the hint of a smile on the man's flinty face.

"I would never put you to such trouble, sir. However, I would like your permission to examine the premises once more, if I may."

"What the devil for?"

Ah, Bradnum thought. I never should have ascribed a sense of humor to the man. To Earle he said, "With the president coming to stay at Elmfield House and the king already in residence, security is our foremost concern. When the president arrives, he will have two constables accompanying him as bodyguards. They will need provisions in terms of a place to sleep, meals, that sort of thing."

Earle's lips formed into a hard line. "I shall arrange it."

"In addition," Bradnum continued, "I should like to station three constables outside on the grounds of Elmfield House. They should not trouble you with the inner workings of your manor, but will provide security in a zone around the estate."

"Will they have to be catered for, too?"

"It would be most helpful if you could provide meals for them so they can stay on duty and not have to be removed from the premises. The men will be rotated in shifts and will not need any sleeping accommodations."

"Well there's a damn silver lining in that cloud."

A quick retort rose in Bradnum's throat, but he choked it down. Instead, he inclined his head in a small bow toward Earle.

"Of course, the constables will be providing security for the king and yourself as well as the president."

Earle snorted. "Don't fill my pockets with bull chips. I know what's important to you and the superintendent. Your damn jobs, that's what. Are you done?"

Bradnum bit the inside of his mouth to keep from lashing out at Earle.

"Yes, sir. I think that covers it."

"Then get out of here and leave me alone. I have an appointment I must keep."

Sweeney pulled the bottom of his waistcoat over the small revolver nestled in his trouser waistband at the small of his back and then knocked lightly on the doorframe of number 210. He bit the inside of his lip as he stood there waiting, trying to look as if he were a house porter summoned on an errand. He knocked again, a bit louder, yet not so loud as to cause a pounding sound at the end of the corridor. Attracting attention was the last thing he wanted.

He was about to knock a third time when the door opened and a skinny young man in wire-rimmed spectacles gave him a bored look.

"The president's room requested assistance in moving furniture," Sweeney began, playing over the rest of his cover story in his mind.

"Not here, partner. Down the hall in number 201. But I can't imagine why they would want to move furniture."

"Sorry to trouble you," Sweeney said, raising a finger to his forehead. The door shut with a loud click of the latch.

Down the hall he knocked forcefully on the door to 201. He could hear footsteps coming toward the door and stepped back as they approached.

"Yes, may I help you?"

The young man standing in the doorway certainly wasn't Roosevelt. Sweeney's mind raced and he could not fathom why he expected the American president to answer his own door.

"I was told that you wanted to have furniture moved in the suite."

A shadow passed across the young man's face. "Please give me a moment to check." Then he shut the door.

Sweeney looked back down the corridor. Still no one about.

Within a minute, the door cracked open a few inches. "Someone has sent you on a wild goose chase. We have no need of furniture being moved here."

The door shut in Sweeney's face with a soft click.

As he stood there in front of the closed door, he could feel the rage rising in his chest. If only he could confront the man. If only he had the president within reach. He knew he could make Roosevelt come to terms with the Irish cause. If only ...

Sweeney spun around at the sound of a door closing at the end of the corridor and watched as a house porter walked toward him, carrying a tray laden with covered dishes. A tide of panic rose from Sweeney's stomach, but he willed it back down and started walking toward the opposite end of the corridor. Coming abreast of the porter, he smiled. "Heavy load, Mate."

The porter nodded. "Eating right hearty up here, they are."

"Like politicians the world around, eh?'

"You'll get no argument from me."

As the porter moved down the hall, Sweeney slipped into the safety of the stairwell."

Madame Chevellier pushed past the thin porter at the door of the Prospect Club and sidestepped nimbly to avoid colliding with a pair of elderly gentlemen making their way out of the private club. She pulled her multi-colored scarf tighter around her shoulders and then angled her black turban to the side of her head. Her hair spilled in controlled disarray down her back. Seeing a wide-eyed cashier behind a polished wood counter set along a side wall, she swished across the carpeted entry hall.

"You will show me to J. R. Earle," she commanded.

The man behind the counter opened his mouth, but no sound came out as he continued to stare bug-eyed at her.

"Are you going to move or will I have to dash around the rooms seeking him for myself?"

The threat of her scuttling around the club apparently was enough to scare the cashier into action.

"I shall locate him for you immediately... Madame." Then he bolted for a doorway at the rear of the entry hall.

Madame Chevellier licked her lips and gazed around the room, returning the stares of the small groups of men who had begun to collect in the room. A few minutes later she heard the gruff growl of J. R. Earle before he descended a wide staircase from the first floor.

"What is this all about? Who the devil are you to pester me in this way?"

Madame Chevellier drew a deep breath and tried to stand taller and straighter, a task complicated by her bulk and weak knees.

"I come to warn you of a great misfortune that will befall you and your company."

Earle turned to the cashier, who stood a pace behind him.

"Do you know this woman?" Earle put a forefinger to his temple and rolled his eyes.

"I am Madame Chevellier, seer of the unknown and foreteller of destinies. You must not take my advice lightly or cast it aside, for I have assisted many people in their times of duress. You may think me mad and make empty gestures, but you will know true despair once the unthinkable happens to your tram company and your guests."

Earle was at the point of turning away to return upstairs when he stopped short and spun toward her.

"Here, now. What do you know about my guests? And what is this... unthinkable?"

The entry hall had become quite crowded during their animated conversation and some of the men looking on pressed closer. The room was as silent as a morgue at midnight.

"You should look to the heavens for the answer, Mr. Earle. The unthinkable will be like a lightning bolt and will transform your company from success to shambles."

Earle's eyes blazed, but she had his full attention.

"And as to your guests, you should see that they are not put in harm's way."

"What the bloody hell is that supposed to mean?"

"I can only tell you what I see in my dreams."

"In your dreams? You expect me to believe the ranting of a madwoman who pushes into a private establishment and ridicules one of its members?"

"I felt it my duty to warn you or impending events. I have done so and will now take my leave."

Madame Chevellier nodded to Earle and turned to leave, but he grabbed her forearm and restrained her.

"You shall pay for your performance here today. You mark me."

She tugged her arm from his grasp and pulled away, her face set in a maniacal mask."

"Mark you? I have foretold of events to come in front of all these witnesses," she said, sweeping her arm in a semi-circle. "When misfortune comes to pass, remember it was I who told you so." Then she swept out of the hall.

Inspector Bradnum trudged up the two flights of stairs to the second floor and emerged into the plushly-carpeted corridor. As he approached the door to room 201, it opened and a house porter emerged with a tray laden with silver dish covers.

"Someone is hungry inside, eh?"

The house porter nodded. Spot of dinner for the folks in there. Are you going in?" He held the door open for Bradnum.

Inside the suite, Robert Wallace stood by a sideboard with a cup of coffee pressed to his lips. He wiped a drop from his lower lip and came over to Bradnum, offering his hand.

"Inspector. It's good to see you again. What brings you to the Grosvenor House?"

Bradnum played with the brim of his hat as he considered his answer. "I believe that I should speak with the president now. Circumstances have developed that have caused us great concern. I should like to discuss the issue of increasing the protective cordon around the president."

Wallace excused himself and went into an adjoining room, returning a few minutes later.

"Please come with me, Inspector."

They went through the doorway into an elaborate sitting room, fitted out with several sofas, two groupings of chairs, and a library table. Roosevelt stood and came from behind the library table, where he had been studying maps.

"Inspector Bradnum," he said, clasping Bradnum's hand in a firm grip. "Thomas has told me of the exemplary work you and your men are doing to protect me and the king."

Roosevelt had a smile that seemed pinned from ear to ear, Bradnum thought. No wonder he is so popular with his countrymen.

"Mr. President. It is a pleasure to meet you. And I must say that we are doing everything in our power to be sure that your visit with us is a safe one."

Bradnum paused, but could see no change on Roosevelt's face.

"I am concerned over recent developments that you and the king may be the focus of some sort of attack during your stay in Hull. I would like to be sure that such a thing does not happen."

Roosevelt leaned forward and clapped Bradnum on the back with a hearty slap.

"I couldn't agree more. What kind of plan do you have in mind? Please sit." Roosevelt waved his hand toward the sofas and chairs.

For the next ten minutes, Bradnum explained the depth of the protection that was in place around the president at the Grosvenor Hotel and the king at Elmfield House. He went into detail about the expanded coverage he planned when

Roosevelt joined the king and Earle. When he finished, he leaned back into the sofa's soft cushions.

"You look as if you could use a drink, Inspector. Do you fancy a finger or two of Scotch — what do you call it over here — whiskey?"

"Aye, Mr. President. But I cannot drink on duty."

"What if the head of a foreign government orders you to have a drink with him?"

Bradnum hesitated only a moment. "Then I must respectfully say... yes, sir."

"Capital! Thomas, bring three glasses of Scotch. We shall drink to the success of this visit. And of course, to my shooting wager with the king."

Bradnum raised his glass to his lips, but the president was quicker, having already drained his glass.

෨

Bradnum leaned against the cool stone at the side of the hotel. He knew he should never have drunk the whiskey with Roosevelt, but what should he have done — refused and caused an incident? This way, no one would know but the three of them, and no one would be talking about it. Right now though, he had to get to Glew's flat to find out what had been happening at the Tramway Depot.

Glew lived in a two-room flat on the second floor of a house on Pryme Street that had seen better days. The building looked indistinguishable from the rest of its neighbors up and down the block — brick facades spanning two-room widths, three stories high, sitting side by side along the entire length of the street.

Bradnum dragged himself up to the top floor and rapped on the doorframe. The door was yanked open almost immediately, and Glew stood there with a blank look on his face.

"Well, let me come in, Glew."

Glew nodded and stood aside. The front room was stuffed with furniture that didn't match. Oak and pine chairs of differing styles were arranged around a scarred pine table. Against one wall was an aged sofa with the stuffing coming out of one arm. Across from it was an ancient leather chair with its covering so cracked that it appeared to be striped.

"What have you found out?" Bradnum asked, lounging against a dark-stained sideboard.

Glew began slowly, stammering and stuttering at first, but as he warmed to his report, he spoke freely, without impediment. When he finished, Bradnum smiled.

"You've done well, Glew. Very well. We shall have to mount a special effort against Mr. Purling. It seems as if he is up to nefarious schemes. I for one would like to know what they are."

"Inspector."

"Yes, Glew."

The constable bit his lip before replying. "Take care with that one. I don't believe he's all there, sir."

Bradnum looked at Glew for a long moment before heading for the door. He wished he had his Brandreth's pills with him.

Chapter Twelve

Teddy Roosevelt puffed his chest out as he emerged from the rear of the touring car that had parked under the carriage portico at the east side of Elmfield House. A double phalanx of servants, most of the men in dark suits and waistcoats and the women in white blouses and long black skirts, applauded as he strode between them and mounted the three steps to the carriage entrance hall.

Elmfield House was laid out in the form of a cross with arms much longer than the post. The main entrance hall formed part of the shorter, northern range of rooms, comprising a sitting room, drawing room and a central hall. South of the hall was the dining room and on either side, billiards and gun rooms. A serving pantry was adjacent to the dining room, and off the pantry were the kitchen, scullery, milk room and larders.

The west and east wings of the house were occupied by a dozen bedrooms, several baths placed strategically on each wing, and an assortment of sitting rooms and garden rooms, each of which provided access to the balustraded patio that wrapped around the building at the back.

As Roosevelt stepped inside, a tall, pinch-faced man in a dark suit stepped forward and offered his hand, introducing himself as J. R. Earle.

"Mr. Earle, I consider it an honor that you've allowed me to be a guest at Elmfield House. I am positively looking forward to seeing all that you have to offer."

Earle harrumphed a laugh. "And we shall offer you a lot, sir."

Off to the side, the king cleared his throat.

"But I am remiss in my introductions," Earle continued smoothly, stepping aside and indicating the king. "May I present His Majesty King Edward VII."

Roosevelt and the king stepped forward simultaneously, clasping hands and locking gazes.

"A monumental pleasure to make your acquaintance, your majesty."

"And yours, Mr. President. Your reputation precedes you... in many ways." The king still held Roosevelt's hand in a tight grip.

A crafty smile crept across Roosevelt's face. "Did my man, Wallace, mention to your staff that I prefer my Dom Perignon chilled quite cold?"

The king smiled broadly in return and released his grasp on Roosevelt's hand. "Apparently you colonials drink your champagne as cold as you do your beer."

"Touché, your majesty. But one can hardly deny the pleasure of a cold draught beer on a steamy summer day."

"I've not had such a pleasure as of yet."

"We shall remedy that situation by having you and the queen visit us in America. After all," he said, eyes twinkling, "you'll want to come over next year and win back the case of Dom Perignon."

The king erupted in a loud laugh. "I was told that you are blunt and cocky. We shall see about the outcome of the wager when we shoot tomorrow."

Roosevelt nodded, and allowed himself to be led down the line and introduced to the rest of the peers and other notables who had gathered at Elmfield House. At the end of the line, he glanced back and saw the king studying him.

Roosevelt winked and clicked his tongue in his cheek twice. "Tomorrow, your majesty. Tomorrow."

Bradnum leaned back in the chair and ran his hands over his face, pulling the fleshy part of his cheeks down as if he were a sad faced hound. He squeezed his eyes together and rubbed his fingertips deeply into the corners of the sockets, pressing against the bone. The previous day had been grueling and he had sought the solace that he often found in smoking opium. He had heeded the warning of the Chinese vendor and only smoked the contents of a single wrapper, but it had been enough to chase away the demons plaguing his head and stomach for the entire night. He had slept a dreamless sleep and found that when he arose with the dawn, a hammering headache was the price he had to pay.

Now, as the headache retreated into a dull ache at the base of his skull, Bradnum grabbed the stack of interrogation reports and began to re-read them. When he finished, something picked at the back of his mind and he cocked his head as if listening to a bird sing in the distance. Crossing to a table strewn with books, reports, letters, telegrams, manacles, a truncheon and other police detritus, he rummaged in a pile of papers and extracted two sheets of paper clipped together.

Bradnum read through the report he had written of the Elmfield House burglary earlier in the year. Then he reviewed the report on Tram Man's assault on a tram rider. Lastly, he scanned the letter Tram Man had sent to the *Graphic's* editor.

He knew there had to be a connection between the elements, but he simply couldn't puzzle out what it was. And then there was the issue of the threats against Roosevelt. The last thing Bradnum wanted was to be the man responsible for letting the American president be harmed. Bradnum dropped the Tram Man letter onto his desk. He would be better off chasing down leads in the Roosevelt case right now. The Tram Man incidents had him stumped.

తా

The king stood in front of the gun room window and sighted down the double barrels of a Holland and Holland 12 bore at an imaginary rising pheasant. "Boom," he said aloud, pushing the word out of his mouth as if he were blowing a bubble. He lowered the gun and drew a deep breath before returning it to the rack set against the wall. Retrieving a Purdy double twelve from the rack, the king repeated the exercise twice more and then cradled the shotgun in his arms, staring out over the garden to the pasture beyond.

A tapping at the door roused him from his reverie.

"Come."

Roosevelt strode into the room, a wide smile creasing his face.

"I thought I might find you here, your majesty. I've had my guns brought down and stored in here." He moved to a gun rack at the far end of the room. Here they are. Perhaps you would care to give them a try." Roosevelt held out a Parker double twelve at arm's length."

The king crossed the room and took the Parker from Roosevelt. He held the Purdy in his left hand."

"You are welcome to try the heft of my Purdy."

Roosevelt stepped two paces away and shouldered the Purdy in a smooth motion, swinging its 28-inch-long barrels in a smooth arc. Then he brought the gun to his eye from a ready position and aimed as if shooting at a rising bird. Slowly, he lowered the muzzled.

"Capital! What a superb handling firearm. The only question we can ask of our firearms is "are we able to shoot as well as they allow us to?""

The king lowered the Parker from his shoulder and cocked his head. "I would hazard a guess that question will be answered at the end of the day tomorrow when the keepers count the bag."

Roosevelt handed the Purdy back to the king and retrieved the Parker.

"Yes, I suppose it will. Let's be sure the keepers can count high."

Then he snapped the Parker to his shoulder and smoothly simulated a shot, making a popping sound with his mouth. He turned to the king and smiled. "I love the taste of champagne.

Patrick Sweeney edged along the iron fence, sheltered from view from anyone inside the estate by the thick stand of boxwood bushes that formed a long border on the other side of the barrier. He turned the corner and found the street ahead of him deserted, now that the day's shadows had lengthened. Quickly he pulled himself to the top of the six-foot-high fence and dropped to the ground on the other side. He considered himself fortunate that the fence tops were flat stubs instead of the usual pointed bars becoming popular. With a measured pace Sweeney moved along the perimeter of the estate, keeping the edifice of Elmfield House in view, but shielding himself from detection by using bushes, trees and in one instance, a gazebo, as cover. He was about to move from behind a grouping of ornamental shrubs when he heard them.

"Anything, Mate?"

"No and I don't believe we shall see a thing all night."

"Well the inspector seems convinced that's something is amiss or he wouldn't have been so forceful about us performing our duties, as he put it."

"My duties should be home in bed with the woman tonight, instead of walking back and forth in J. R. Earle's garden."

"But the king and the American president count on us to protect them."

The sound of a harsh laugh reached Sweeney's ears.

"They've nothing to fear. There's nothing out there but rabbits eating the bloody flowers."

Sweeney eavesdropped on the two men until their voices began to fade and he took the opportunity to slowly peer around the bush. They had separated and walked in different directions, each carrying a foot-long wooden truncheon on a leather lanyard. They were dressed in civilian clothes, but Sweeney could spot a policeman from a block away. He stared hard at the policeman nearest him. There seemed to be a large lump in the man's coat pocket. It was unlikely that he was carrying his supper hidden there. The lump had to be a revolver.

Sweeney backed away into the shadows and made his way back to the fence the way he had come.

"Bloody hell, he thought. "Now they're bound to be everywhere. I'll have to find a way around the buggers."

❧

Richard Purling watched the tram turn onto Chanterlands Avenue where it ran through Hull Western Cemetery toward the outer limits of the track system. Once he was sure the tram was well on its way down the street, he emerged from behind the bushes and walked briskly to catch up with the passenger who had left the tram at the intersection. As he approached from behind, Purling could see that the man was elderly, shrouded in a long coat, and walked with the assistance of an ebony-handled cane.

Purling timed his approach to come abreast of the man when he was deep in shadows between street lamps on the quiet road. The man turned at hearing his tread, but Purling pushed into him and pulled a black hood over the man's head, tightening the ends around his throat. The old man's feet slipped out from under him and as he fell he struck out with his cane, splitting the skin at Purling's hairline.

Blood dripped from Purling's forehead and splattered on the old man's overcoat as he thrashed on the ground, but Purling held a strong grip on the ends of the hood and pulled tighter. In less than a minute the old man stopped moving. Purling held his grip until he was certain the old man was dead and then removed the hood.

From the inner pocket of his jacket he extracted a paper that he unfolded and slipped inside the front of the old man's coat. Then he stood, and after checking the street in both directions, pulled himself over the chest-high cemetery wall and disappeared into the gloom.

Chapter Thirteen

The heavy pounding wrenched Bradnum from a deep sleep and he plodded to the door to put a stop to the noise.

"What in the hell is it?" he growled, yanking the door open.

A burly police constable filled the doorway. "Beggin' yer pardon, Inspector, but there's been a murder. I've been sent to fetch you."

Bradnum dragged a hand over his eyes and across his mouth.

"Why at this time of night? Wouldn't it keep 'til morning?"

"The duty sergeant said ye'd want to see this one, sir."

"And why is that?"

"It's council member Ascot, Inspector. And then there's the note on the body."

"The note?"

"Aye. From Tram Man himself."

Bradnum splashed water on his face from the washstand basin and dressed hurriedly. Within a half hour, he and the constable arrived at Bank West in front of Hull Western Cemetery. The constables had cordoned off the murder scene with hemp rope that ran from the cemetery wall to a horse-drawn wagon standing in the road, along the street to a two-seat police car and then back to the wall. The area was lit by more than a dozen large lanterns. A sergeant detached himself from a small knot of policeman and came over as Bradnum got out of his vehicle.

"Apologies for dragging you out of a warm bed, Inspector, but I was sure you would want to see this for yourself." He gestured to the body laying across the pavement.

Bradnum approached the dead man.

"Was this the manner in which the victim was found?" he asked.

The sergeant stepped closer and made a face. "No sir. When the first constable arrived, he noticed a paper sticking out of the front of the man's coat. The constable opened the coat and read the note, which is why we summoned you."

"Are we absolutely sure that it is Mr. Ascot of the council?"

"Positively. I know the man and that is definitely him. Poor buggar."

Bradnum pulled a handkerchief from his pocket and picked up the note by a corner. He tilted it to catch the light and read aloud.

FOR THE HULL POLICE:

I WARNED PEEPLE THRU THE GRAPHIC TO STAY OFF THE TRAMS. THEY DID NOT LISSEN SO I KILLS THIS CONCIL MAN TO MAKE THEM KNOW WHAT HAPPENS. BECAUSE JR EARLE DOES NOT HELP HIS WORKERS. I WILL DO MORE HARM IN COMING DAYS. I HEER YOU CALL ME TRAM MAN NOW. HA HA

ZEUS

"Christ, just what I wanted to see in the middle of the night," Bradnum grouched. Turning to the sergeant, he said, "Have the constable who found the body report to me. I would like to question him. Has Doctor Rawson examined the body yet?"

"Yes sir. He has come and gone."

"Splendid. Then have the corpse removed to the morgue for the postmortem. I expect that with those ligature marks around his neck we shall be told he was strangled to death."

"Anything else, Inspector?"

Bradnum rubbed his stomach, which rumbled noisily.

"Yes. One more thing. See if you can find some Eno's Fruit Salts for me." He stifled a belch. It was going to be a long night.

❧

The morning dawned cool and clear, with only wisps of high clouds scudding across the sky. Teddy Roosevelt stood at the open window with the drapes drawn aside, breathing deeply and exhaling noisily, all the while watching the sun appear over the treed horizon. He turned at the sound of rapping on his door.

"Robert, what a delightful morning. Come over here and take in a lungful or two of this wonderful country air."

"Thank you, Mr. President, but I've already been outside to speak with the keepers."

Roosevelt cocked his head. "The keepers? And what have they to say?"

Wallace smiled thinly. "Only that the king is a crack shot and that you shall have your work cut out for you if you're to best him in this contest. The wager between the two of you is all that anyone on the estate is talking about."

Roosevelt's teeth gleamed whitely as he smiled. "Bully for them! I hope they put their money on the right man."

"It appears that the wagering amongst the staff is running two to one in favor of the king."

The president threw back his head and laughed. "You had better snatch some of those wagers for yourself, Robert. I daresay you could make quite a killing, so to speak."

"I shall keep that in mind, sir. Will you be taking breakfast here or downstairs with the others?"

Roosevelt stretched his arms overhead and turned back to the window. "Downstairs, Robert. No sense in denying the English a closer look at their colonial betters."

A half hour later, Roosevelt strolled into the dining room and all conversation ceased at the table as a dozen pair of eyes watched him enter.

"Gentlemen, please. Don't let me interrupt your discussions," Roosevelt said, sitting in a chair at the midpoint of the table. "Your Majesty, I trust you are well."

The king, at the head of the table, nodded and smiled slowly. "You slept well, I take it? We certainly would not want anything spoiling your aim today."

Roosevelt sat back as he was served from a silver tray. "My aim is the same every day, your majesty. Dead on."

The king's face remained a pleasant mask. "Yes, well, I suppose it will all come down to that later today."

As breakfast wore on, the conversation at the table moved from shooting to politics to international events. Lord Roseberry, a septuagenarian with twinkling blue eyes who sat across from Roosevelt, leaned forward.

"Mr. President, perhaps you could tell us of your adventure on the rail line from Liverpool. It is said there was an explosion on the line."

Roosevelt squared his shoulders and looked directly at Lord Roseberry.

"Nothing to worry about, my lord. There is plenty of unpleasantness in the world. Regrettably, some of it took place not far from here on a railroad siding. But I am reliably informed that no one was injured and only rolling stock was damaged. Rail cars can always be replaced, can't they?"

Roosevelt raised his coffee cup to the group. "Gentlemen. Enough talk of trivial matters. Here's to good shooting."

ॐ

The headline on the special early afternoon edition of the *Hull Graphic* screamed off the front page in two-inch-high black headlines.

COUNCIL MEMBER ASCOT

MURDERED

MYSTERIOUS NOTE FOUND ON BODY

The article, carrying the byline of Albert Leake, continued in a similar vein.

> Last night a dastardly murder was perpetrated upon one of Hull's distinguished and longstanding council members, Edwin Ascot. Mr. Ascot was found on the north pavement of Bank West, adjacent to the Hull West Cemetery. Police sources tell the *Graphic* that it appears Mr. Ascot had been strangled.
>
> One of the more curious aspects of the case is the appearance of a note that was found tucked into Mr. Ascot's overcoat, assumedly after his death. While we were not told of the contents of the note, a constable did confirm that the note was

addressed to the police, made further threats against the citizens of Hull, and was signed by the Tram Man.

Interested readers will remember that the villain who has come to be called 'Tram Man' has in the past communicated with the *Graphic's* editors in the hope of stating his case to the public. Apparently Tram Man has grievances with the Hull Tramway Company in general and the managing director, Mr. J. R. Earle, in particular.

The Tram Man has taken responsibility for causing several accidents along the tram lines and also of assaulting passengers after they use the trams.

The police have had no luck in catching Tram Man thus far. Inspector Herbert Bradnum is in charge of the case and continues to say that the police are investigating all avenues that might lead them to the apprehension of their man. But to this point, it has all been for naught.

The news account went on for many more paragraphs, rehashing the accidents along the tram lines that were ascribed to the Tram Man, as well as those assaults on the unfortunate citizens who had used the tram system and been assaulted after exiting the trams. The article concluded ominously.

Many in the city are asking the obvious question of the police: When will Tram Man be caught so that citizens can again feel safe in the confines of their town? To this point, the police have no answer to that question.

&

The sun had begun to slip well toward the horizon when the last drive of the day started. The beaters that the keepers had hired moved through the thick underbrush on the back acreage of the estate, making as much noise as they could in order to flush any pheasants lurking under the cover. As a handful of beaters moved up out of a depression laced with thick cover toward an open field, a trio of pheasant ran and then exploded into the air in front of Roosevelt.

The president raised his Parker smoothly to his shoulder and took the first bird down at head height. He continued swinging the double barrel gun from right to left and centered the second pheasant on the barrel's gold bead.

Blam! The report of the shotgun split the air and the second pheasant tumbled to the ground.

Almost as soon as Roosevelt had pulled the trigger on the second bird, another shot rang out from his left. The king had pulled down on the third pheasant flushed and dropped it into the field as it had tried to gain enough height to escape.

Roosevelt lowered his Parker and looked over at the king, who still was looking toward the bird he had shot, when two near simultaneous shots sounded and the ground in between the two of them was rent with lead shot.

Roosevelt threw himself to the ground, sprawled out alongside a small rock outcropping. When no further shots were fired, he stood and brushed himself off.

"What the hell was that all about?"

A keeper ran up to Roosevelt and touched his cap. "Mr. President, please come this way." He led Roosevelt toward a fold in the ground where the king had already been taken.

"Theodore, are you all right?" the king asked.

"Fine. I might ask the same of you."

"I am untouched. Those shots..." the king began. "Do you think they were meant for us?"

Roosevelt raised up on his toes and peered over the edge of the depression where they stood hidden.

"I don't think they were for the birds, your Majesty."

&

William Cole edged into Bradnum's office and stood in front of the inspector's desk wringing his cap in his hands. Bradnum thought he looked like a schoolboy called into the headmaster's office for a rules infraction.

"The sergeant tells me that you have information about what the papers call the Tram Man case. Is that correct?"

Cole nodded his head and a thick lock of dark hair fell across his eyes. He brushed it back. "Aye, Inspector. I am acquainted with a man called Richard Purling, an electrical engineer at the tram depot where I work."

Bradnum motioned him to sit. "And what is your position at the tramway?"

"A driver, sir. I believe you spoke to me at a derailment on Charlotte Street near the Queen's Dock some months ago."

Bradnum rose and raised a forefinger in front of his face. "I remember you now. You were most helpful with details of the accident scene." He angled his head and peered at Cole. "What do you have to say now?"

"Only that I am certain that Richard... Purling, I mean to say... is planning something very unpleasant for the owners of the tramway."

Bradnum straightened and pinched his eyebrows. "Very unpleasant, you say. Would you care to elaborate for me?"

"It's like this, Inspector. Richard is an excellent engineer. He knows more about the properties of electricity than anyone else in the town, probably in the entire county. But he has been very secretive of late and spends more and more of his time in the electrical generating shed, even to the point of neglecting the maintenance on the trams. And that is one of his chief responsibilities."

"I don't see how this relates to the case."

Cole squirmed in the chair. "I don't know how to say this, sir, so I'll simply come out with it. I believe that Richard is Tram Man."

Bradnum sat down and stared at Cole for several seconds before speaking. "Please tell me what makes you come to that conclusion?"

Cole took a deep breath and exhaled loudly. "You see, Richard has always been an unusual individual. Goes his own way, if you get my drift. But I have what you might characterize as a friendship with him, although I think it is more because of my efforts than his. In any event, he has been unusually reticent of late and much more vociferous in his railings against the world in general and J. R. Earle in particular. Richard believes that the tram company, and specifically Mr. Earle, treat the company employees badly. I cannot say that I agree with him. I think he has some type of limitation on his brain that causes him to think unclearly. That is the only answer that I can suggest for his unusual viewpoints and behaviors."

"And what would these behaviors include?"

Cole drew another deep breath. "As I said earlier, he spends an inordinate amount of time in the electric generating shed, which he has never done in the past. He also has an assistant now, a Mr. Glew, to whom he seems to have attached himself as a professor would fasten onto a potential protégé. And from what Richard has told me in snippets of conversation, I believe that he prowls the tram lines at night. For what purpose, I cannot say."

Bradnum stared at Cole for a half-minute without saying anything. As if awaking from a daydream, he asked, "Was there any other point to which you would like to draw my attention?"

Cole shook his head. "No sir. That's the lot of it."

Bradnum jumped to his feet, smiling. "Well I must thank you for your candor, Mr. Cole," he said, extending his hand. "I shall find you at the tram depot if I have any further questions."

ॐ

Roosevelt entered the billiards room and headed toward the king, who was deep in conversation with his private secretary in front of the French doors. At his approach, the king said something nearly inaudible to Taylor, who nodded and excused himself.

"What news of the mysterious shots this afternoon?"

The king leveled his gaze at Roosevelt and took a long sip from the short tumbler he held. "A whiskey, first, perhaps?" he asked, and when Roosevelt nodded, the king snapped his fingers in the direction of a servant standing against the wall.

When Roosevelt had a whiskey in hand and the king's drink had been refreshed, the president tried again. "Edward, you are not being very forthcoming with details."

The king sighed heavily. "Theodore, you are a man used to the travails of the military life and have had the experience of being shot at before. Without result, fortunately. I have not been in such a situation until today and it has unsettled me."

Roosevelt sipped the whiskey and smacked his lips. "By god, that is tasty." He leaned forward toward the king. "Eventually, you shall come to look at this incident as simply another event in your long life. And yes, I can sympathize with you about the effect being shot at produces in a man. The thing to remember is that whoever was behind the trigger, missed. We can be thankful he was a bad shot. I assume your men caught him?"

The king leaned back into the folds of the chair, causing the leather to squeak. "My men were not able to locate the shooter."

Roosevelt's eyebrows arched. "Edward, he had to have been within 50 yards or closer to us. How could they not catch him?"

"Their first concern was for our safety, so they hustled you and me into that dip in the field. Only after they saw us safe did it occur to my chief man to search for the perpetrator. He was able to determine that the shots came from a small copse of trees to the west. By the time he arrived there and examined the surrounding area, the shooter had gone."

"There was no sign of him?"

"Only one or two bootprints. And these." The king drew a pair of shotgun cartridge casings from his waistcoat pocket. He passed them over to Roosevelt.

"Twelve bore casings," Roosevelt said, holding them up to the light. "And it appears they were filled with double zero shot, if this marking on the side is correct."

The king nodded. "Aye. What do you Americans call it?'

Roosevelt leveled his gaze on the king. "Double-ought buckshot. It's generally used to bring down deer-sized game. I suppose it would serve well on human-sized targets as well."

The king shuddered and took another sip before turning to the servant. "Find Mr. Taylor and ask him to step into the billiards room."

The king's private secretary appeared five minutes later, dressed in a black suit and white shirt that looked as if they were brand new.

"Taylor, have you been able to tally the results of the shoot this afternoon?"

"Yes, your majesty. I have it right here." He pulled a paper from his inside jacket pocket and unfolded it before handing it to the king.

"That will be all for now, Thomas."

When Taylor had gone, the king smiled thinly at Roosevelt. "You are desirous of knowing the bag results, Theodore?"

"By thunder, you know very well I am. What are they?"

The king handed him the paper. "I shot 57 birds and you bagged 62. I suppose I owe you a case of Dom Perignon.

Roosevelt smiled broadly and extended his hand to the king. "I shall think of you each time I open a bottle.

Chapter Fourteen

Inspector Bradnum's boots crunched on the gravel drive as he walked toward the main entrance of Elmfield House. The duty sergeant had sent a constable to awaken him at midnight and tell him of the attempt against the king and the president. Try as he might, he couldn't fall asleep after that bit of news and spent the balance of the night pondering the improbabilities in this case.

A well-tailored butler led him along the main corridor of the house and showed him into a sunny conservatory where the king, Roosevelt and Earle stood examining a grouping of orchids.

"Inspector. Good of you to come by," the king said. "Dastardly business."

"Your majesty. Mr. President. I have been informed that both of you are unharmed."

"Unharmed, but getting damned angry with whoever is behind these attempts," Roosevelt said.

"Yes sir, I can understand why you would be angry. But I have questions I would like to pose so I can get on with the investigation."

"The bloody police have been unable to find anyone responsible for all that has happened thus far," boomed

Earle. "What makes you think you shall be any help in this situation?"

Bradnum started to formulate a defensive answer, but was interrupted by the king, who said, "Tell us what you need to know."

"Mr. Earle, were there any new faces among the keepers on the estate?"

Earle pushed out his lower lip and shook his head. "Nay. They have all been with me for years."

"How about among the beaters used to drive the pheasant?"

Earle exploded. "How the hell should I know the background of every common worker who comes onto my estate. You can assume there were plenty of new faces among them."

Bradnum kept his temper in check. "I shall require a list of the names of those individuals used as beaters."

Earle glowered at Bradnum. "I shall have my man get it for you. Anything else?"

"Your Majesty, did you notice anyone among the shooting parties who appeared not to belong there or not to fit in with the crowd?"

"No, I cannot say that I did."

"Mr. President, how about you?"

"Inspector, I was watching for the birds, not the beaters."

"Understandable, sir. But perhaps you might have noticed something that escaped your attention during the shoot."

Earle interrupted. "This is a waste of time. Are you not done yet?"

"J. R., let the inspector finish," the king said gently.

"Now that you bring it up," the president said, "there was a young lad among the beaters who seemed to keep well apart from the others when we stopped for a rest."

"Can you describe him?"

"Short, slim, about nineteen or twenty years old. And he had a shock of red hair and freckles. Looked like an Irish lad."

Bradnum looked from one man to the other and finally snapped his notebook shut. "Gentlemen, thank you for your time. I shall not be troubling you further this morning."

Outside Elmfield House, as Bradnum was getting into his car, a small two-seat Wolseley car drew up beside him. Albert Leake stepped out and touched the brim of his hat.

"Morning, Inspector. Would you care to give me a comment about the Tram Man case, or perhaps you would like to address the unexplained shooting at the king and the president?"

Bradnum ground his teeth and clenched his fists, but then forced himself to relax.

"Leaky, you really should take a bit more time in preparing your stories so you get the facts right."

"The facts are that the police are at a standstill on the Tram Man case. And my guess is that you shall be in similar circumstances concerning this shooting."

Like a bowstring snapping under too much pressure, Bradnum's patience broke. He grabbed Leake by the collar and the scruff of his pants and propelled him back through the still-open driver's door of the Wolseley, releasing him to sprawl across the seat and bump his head into the opposite door.

Bradnum pickup up the notepad Leake had dropped and tossed it into the car.

"Do not return until you find a civil tongue in your head," he said.

༺

Bradnum watched the chief keeper shift from foot to foot and finally lean against the wall of the bird shed at the back of the estate, his fingers plucking at the fabric of his cord trousers. The shed was a three-sided roofed enclosure that provided the keepers a measure of protection from the elements as they tallied the animals taken during a hunt and then cleaned the carcasses in preparation for going to the kitchen. Bradnum moved in closer to the keeper.

"Dutton, isn't it?"

The keeper nodded, still plucking at his leg.

Bradnum smiled through pressed lips. "How many keepers were out among the crowd yesterday?"

"Three keepers. Four counting me, sir."

"And the number of beaters?"

"Oh, much greater, sir." The keeper looked toward the roof of the shed as if the number of beaters were somehow written there for him to see. He rolled his eyes back down to look at Bradnum. "Nearly four dozen sir."

"All from the estate?"

The keeper shook his head. "Nay. We cannot keep so many on staff, so we use men from the town. Men who have beat for us before."

"And was that the case yesterday. All men who beat for you in the past."

Dutton looked at the ground and scraped his boot heel in the dirt. "Nay, I cannot say they did."

Bradnum cocked his head and stared hard at the keeper. "I am sure you would like to explain what you mean."

The keeper drew a deep breath before answering. "We had to have another dozen beaters for the hunt, as it was such a large one. We are not used to pushing that many birds from cover all at the same time." He pulled at the corners of his mouth. "I called on an acquaintance at the Old Mill Public House and had him send over some men who had worked as beaters before."

Bradnum took a step back, keeping his gaze on Dutton. "And the man's name?"

"Loughrey. Shamus Loughrey. You'll find him at the Old Mill pub in the evenings."

Bradnum put his forefinger to his lips. "Not a word, Mr. Dutton. Nothing. Do I make myself clear?"

Dutton hung his head and nodded. "Aye. You do."

❧

Richard Purling splashed the tepid water on his face from the wash basin and swore silently as it splashed down the front of his trousers. He snatched a threadbare cloth from the wooden rack above the washstand and quickly soaked up the liquid on his pants and then returned to soaking his whiskers. When he was satisfied that the stubble on his face was soft enough, he wet a worn shaving brush in the basin and then swirled his vigorously on the thin cake of shaving soap. When he had enough lather, he leaned close to the small mirror on the wall and carefully painted his face with the lather. Stropping the straight razor several times to hone its edge, he held it up to the light before applying it to his face in a long, broad stroke.

When he finished shaving, Purling rinsed his face and shook out a few drops of the precious lavender scent that he had saved for special occasions. He grimaced as the liquid stung his scraped cheeks, but forced himself to smile at the reflection in the mirror.

"You shall have a fine time tonight with those who consider themselves your betters," he said to the reflection. "And they shall see exactly who they are up against."

Purling studied himself for a minute before turning to the narrow bed where he had laid out the rest of the suit of clothes he would wear that evening. He got into the stiff white shirt and fumbled with the wrist and neck fastenings, finally securing them with another silent curse. He next put on the plain black waistcoat, and buttoning it carefully. Last, he shrugged into the jacket that was too long in the sleeves and a bit big in the shoulders. He had purchased the jacket at a second-hand store three blocks away and was not happy with the fit at the time, and yet could do nothing about it. Purling puffed out his chest and then turned sideways to look at his profile in the small mirror.

"It will have to do," he said to his reflection, before leaving the dingy room.

੭

The Old Mill Public House stood on the site of a medieval flour mill that was abandoned after the course of the stream it straddled dwindled and eventually dried up. The mill itself fell into disrepair until an enterprising stranger from one of the southern counties arrived in town with enough money and enthusiasm to buy the structure and try to rehabilitate it, not as a mill, but as a public house. Sitting near a major crossroads on the outskirts of Hull, and not far down the road from Elmfield House, the Old Mill Public House quickly became a social focal point for the area and remained as popular as when it was rebuilt.

Inspector Bradnum pushed open the heavy pub door and stepped into the smoky haze in the large front room, stopping for a moment to let his eyes adjust to the gloom. Seeing the publican at the end of the long bar, Bradnum threaded his way through throngs of patrons and squeezed into a spot at the bar's end. When the publican approached, he showed his warrant card and leaned across the bar.

"I would like a word with you about one of your patrons."

The publican's eyebrows rose and he scanned the bar room. "There's lot of them here tonight."

"I am only interested in one of them. Shamus Loughrey."

Bradnum saw the publican's gaze flicker to the back of the bar room, to a table in a corner where a sandy haired, middle aged man sat along, a mug of beer on the table in front of him.

"Is that Loughrey?" Bradnum asked, cocking his head toward the corner.

The publican nodded so slightly that anyone watching would have failed to notice.

Bradnum raised his hand in acknowledgement and moved across the room. He pulled a stool out from under the table and sat.

"Fancy a bit of company?"

Loughrey stared hard at him. "Who might you be?"

"Only a man seeking information."

"Try the reading rooms over on Hever Street," Loughrey snapped. "They have plenty of books there for getting information."

Bradnum sighed heavily and produced his warrant card. "Inspector Bradnum. And you would be Shamus Loughrey, I believe."

"You would be right in believing that."

"Have you heard anything about what took place at Elmfield House this afternoon?"

Loughrey stiffened. "I know nothing of the place."

"Then you did not supply a dozen beaters to the chief keeper there?"

Loughrey opened his mouth to speak, but must have thought better of it. He said nothing.

"I already have a statement from Dutton that you procured a dozen beaters to supplement those he usually uses for pheasant drives on the estate. If you are having difficulty remembering that arrangement with Mr. Dutton, perhaps we should step along to the police station where we can continue this discussion."

Loughrey snatched his mug from the table and swallowed half its contents, putting the mug back on the table with a shaky hand. "What if I did supply beaters for the hunt? There's no crime in that."

"Ah, that is where you are wrong," Bradnum said, waggling his forefinger. "You see, one of the men you put on that estate took shots at the king and the American president."

Loughrey's eyes grew wide and his mouth formed into a circle as he sucked in air. "Oh, Christ."

"He will not be able to help you now, Mr. Loughrey. The man we are seeking is about nineteen or twenty, of Irish descent, with a shock of red hair and plenty of freckles. Does that description sound familiar to you?"

"The stupid shit."

"I am sure that cannot be his name, Mr. Loughrey."

Loughrey exhaled loudly and stared at Bradnum for a long moment. "All right. His name is Billy Behan. You can find him in lodgings on Atwood Street."

"Very well. Finish your beer, Mr. Loughrey. You and I are going to the station to continue this chat. And then I shall go and see Mr. Behan."

Chapter Fifteen

Bradnum looked at the address he had penciled on a scrap of paper and then peered down the row of dilapidated houses lining Atwood Street. He was two blocks away from the sawmills that flanked the enormous Victoria Dock and its adjacent timber ponds and yet the smell of freshly-sawn timber stuck in his nose. He found number 28 halfway down the street, a three story wood and stone house, with hanging shutters and badly in need of paint. Next to it was a narrow alley leading to a dingy courtyard in the rear.

As he stepped into the courtyard, two dirty children scampered away from him, but not before he caught the nearest by the collar and lifted him off the ground. Bradnum held the boy at arm's length, keeping his windmilling feet a safe distance away.

"Run, Benny. Run. He'll get you for sure," the boy called to his companion, who disappeared into a narrow space between two sheds.

"Easy, boy," Bradnum said. "I mean you no harm."

The boy stopped kicking. "I knows a copper when I sees one."

"Since you are such an observant lad, perhaps you can help me. I am looking for a young man called Billy Behan who lives in the court. Can you tell me where he might be?"

The boy eyed Bradnum warily. "Wot's it worth for me?"

Bradnum smiled as he set the boy on the ground. "Tuppence."

The boy folded his arms across his chest and looked away from Bradnum. Turning back, he said, "Sixpence."

Bradnum shook his head. "Thruppence will have to suffice."

"Done."

The boy held out his hand for the coin, but Bradnum held it back. "The information first."

The boy pointed to a doorway at the bottom of a short staircase to a cellar. "Down there. We calls him 'rat boy' on account of he's always catchin' rats."

Bradnum pressed the coin into the boy's outstretched palm and watched him scuttle away into the same hole into which his friend had squeezed.

Hitching up his pants, Bradnum approached the cellar door and rapped hard on it three times. He could hear someone moving inside and took a half-step back as the door swung open to reveal a red-haired, heavily-freckled young man of about twenty.

"Billy Behan?"

"And who wants to know?"

Bradnum held out his warrant card and introduced himself. "You can tell me what you know about the shooting at Elmfield House here and now, or we can talk about it at the police station. It's your choice, lad."

"What if I've nothing to say?"

Bradnum sucked in his lower lip. "That would be a bit difficult for me to believe. We know you were employed on the estate as a beater for the king's hunt. You were seen near the woods when the shots were fired at the king and the president. And Shamus Loughrey himself confirms that he supplied you with an old double twelve bore. He says you haven't returned it. Shall I come inside and have a look for it?"

Behan's eyes had widened as Bradnum talked, and the inspector slipped his foot over the threshold in case the boy tried to slam the door. But Behan appeared to deflate as his shoulders sagged and he pushed the door open.

"You may as well come in. You will anyway."

Bradnum followed him into the small, shabby room, its only furniture a rickety chair, a scarred wood table and a straw mattress set on a wooden frame. Bradnum looked around the room and bent down at the end of the bed frame, reaching under it. He extracted, butt first, a double barrel hammer gun.

"Would this be the shotgun we were just discussing?"

Behan hung his head and nodded.

Bradnum set the gun down on the bed and took hold of the boy's forearm.

"Billy Behan, I am placing you under arrest for making an attempt on the lives of the king of England and the American president."

⌇

The Waltham Street Hotel stood to the northeast of the six-way intersection of Jameson, King Edward, Waltham. West, Story and Chariot Streets. The hotel had been erected 50 years earlier on the east side of Waltham Street, two buildings north of the intersection. In the intervening years, the hotel management purchased the buildings to the south and renovated the spaces so the hotel had a presence on the busy intersection, only a block north of City Hall.

In the course of renovations, the hotel installed a magnificent ballroom on the first floor, where it was able to seat five hundred guests for formal dinner at a single serving. The room was lit by glittering chandeliers made by LeGrande, one of the finest makers in Paris, and its broadloom carpet was deep purple, the color of royalty. When the heavy drapes were pulled back from the windows fronting the hotel, guests could look down the length of King Edward Street to the statue of the late queen in Queen Victoria Square.

Waltham Street Hotel was the place that Teddy Roosevelt chose to host a reception for King Edward VII and as many of Hull's notable citizens as could be gathered in the ballroom.

Roosevelt, ever the amiable host, stood at the center of a knot of well-wishers not far from one of the of several bars placed strategically throughout the ballroom, finishing the story of how he had dropped two pheasant with a single shot.

"Those birds rose from the bracken almost as one," he said, "but I was ready for them. I had heard them running over there and was facing toward them, with my gun at the ready." Roosevelt raised his hand to his mouth and kissed the inside of his fist with a loud smack. "It was a thing of beauty to see. The two pheasant rising hard, trying to get enough speed up to escape. And there I was, standing ready, my gun's muzzles already swinging onto them, leading them just a little bit because they were moving so slowly. And then, Blam, Blam." He shrugged his shoulders. "Down they went."

Someone at the rear of the group raised his glass. "To President Roosevelt."

Hands raised glasses and voices called, nearly in unison, "To the president."

As they finished the toast, a herald at the ballroom's entrance stood to attention and bugled a call on his horn.

"His majesty has arrived," someone said.

All eyes turned toward the ballroom entrance as King Edward VII stepped through the wide doorway, resplendent in a military uniform, his chest covered with ribbons and medals. The king made his way through to the center of the ballroom, nodding to well-wishers, speaking a word or two to several people. As he traversed the room, the group in front of Roosevelt parted and the king walked straight up to the president. The king smiled, showing very white teeth.

"Well, Theodore. I can tell you it is an extreme pleasure to be honored by you at this reception." The king gestured around the room. "So many good friends and acquaintances are here. I am very pleased."

Roosevelt inclined his head to the king. "Your majesty. The night is yours. I am pleased to be your host. There is only one thing I must ask."

The king's eyebrows lifted in surprise. "And what might that be?"

Roosevelt winked. "That you don't forget the case of Dom Perignon you owe me."

For a moment the king looked blankly on, and then broke out into laughter.

"Theodore, you are incorrigible."

As he spoke, a commotion broke out near the ballroom's entrance. Roosevelt looked over and saw a small man with a shock of unruly hair struggling with J. R. Earle. The man seemed intent on coming into the reception and Earle seemed just as intent on keeping him out. After a minute of pushing back and forth, a burly man in evening clothes and a constable took hold of the small man by his arms and ushered him out of the ballroom.

Earle brushed off his dinner jacket and was joined by a man that Roosevelt recognized as Inspector Bradnum. The pair sauntered across the room to where the king and Roosevelt chatted quietly.

"Damn fool," Earle boomed. "I told him he wasn't welcome here."

"Who was he and what did he want?" Roosevelt asked.

"He's the bloody buggar who tells the lies to the *Graphic*," Earle said. "Lies and more lies."

Bradnum coughed politely, "He also is a person who we are very interested in," he said. "The police, that is."

Roosevelt eyed him for a moment. "Why are you interested in him? Does it have anything to do with this business between the king and me?"

"Not that we know at this point, Mr. President. I can tell you, however, that we are most anxious to get more information from Mr. Purling — that is his name, Richard Purling — about the case everyone is now calling the Tram Man case."

"Damn foolish name for a serious problem," Earle chimed in. "Who the devil put that label on it, I want to know."

Bradnum looked at Earle as if he had grown an extra head. "Why the *Graphic*, of course."

‌‍⤏

Madame Chevellier stretched her shoulders back and allowed the cleft in her ample bosom to attract the attention of the houseman at the ballroom door. She squeezed Samuel Owst's arm a bit tighter as they stepped carefully down the carpeted staircase leading to the main floor and the throng of people milling around. She could hear snatches of hushed conversation as she passed and smiled when she realized they were talking about her.

Owst stopped short near a tall, hatchet faced man who stood alone next to a pinch-faced, gray haired woman.

"William, it's good to see you." Owst turned to the small woman next to him. "Mrs. Higgins. My pleasure. I am Samuel

Owst, the editor of the *Graphic,* and this is Madame Chevellier, the distinguished psychic."

Mrs. Higgins forced a smile and nodded to each of them in turn.

Madame Chevellier couldn't resist the challenge. She extended her hand, palm down, toward Higgins, practically forcing him to grasp her fingers and brush his lips across them, each of which adorned by a large ring capped by a colored gemstone.

"What a gallant man you have, Mrs. Higgins," she said, smiling tightly.

Mrs. Higgins muttered something inaudible, but was rescued by her husband.

"Samuel, have you met the king and the president yet?" he asked.

Owst craned his neck to see through the crowd. "We've only just arrived and it appears there is a considerable line formed for that very pleasure," he said. "Would you care to join us?"

"I think not," Mrs. Higgins said quickly. "We already have paid our respects."

"Then we should be doing so ourselves," Madame Chevellier shot back, her eyes bright. "Samuel, we should present ourselves." She turned back to Mrs. Higgins. "Mind you care for that wonderful man, won't you?" Just as quickly, she pulled on Owst's arm and led him to the end of the reception line.

"Was that necessary?" he asked.

"Samuel, I do appreciate your bringing me to this reception, but I must not suffer fools lightly. That woman's aura was as dark as a summer thundercloud. I simply tried to point out one of the positive elements in her life."

Owst laughed, shaking his head. "You do continue to amaze me," he said. "Are you not aware of the controversy you cause when you perform like that?"

Madame Chevellier leaned away from him. "Perform?" she asked, her eyebrows arched. "That is what I do every day of my life, just as you do."

Owst stared at her for a long moment and then the two of them burst into laughter.

It was nearly fifteen minutes later before they found themselves at the head of the reception line, headed by J. R. Earle.

"Samuel, delighted you could come," Earle said, pumping Owst's hand. "And who is this lovely creature?"

Owst introduced her to Earle and she nearly winced as he kissed her knuckles in the French fashion. Earle turned to the king, standing to his right.

"Your majesty, may I present Samuel Owst, the editor of the *Hull Graphic*."

Owst bowed and the king nodded. "Good of you to come, Owst."

Madame Chevellier then stepped in front of the king, and curtseyed, as Earle introduced her. The king seemed disinterested.

She stepped to the left and found herself in front of Roosevelt. Robert Wallace's voice floated up from behind the president, introducing her. She curtseyed again and as she came up, saw Roosevelt offering his hand.

"Mr. President," she said, grasping his hand in hers, "it is such a pleasure to meet you. I have read so many complimentary articles about you."

Roosevelt laughed, but did not take his hand away. "You must not be reading the same newspapers that I do."

As his gaze locked on hers, she felt the familiar power surging over her. "Mr. President," she said as she pressed her hand more tightly into his, "you must be very careful in the next several days. Trouble awaits you."

Roosevelt's eyes flared. "Trouble seems to find me wherever I go,"

She shook her head slowly, running her index finger along the lifeline in his right palm. "This trouble is very close, sir, and I fear it is trouble that will be difficult to avoid."

Roosevelt took a deep breath and broke their connection, dropping his hand to his side.

"Madame, I always have been ready for whatever Fate has in store for me. It has been a pleasure meeting you."

When Madame Chevellier and Owst had cleared the reception line and stood next to a massive Ionic style column near the front of the ballroom, Owst leaned close to her ear.

"What was that all about, the business about trouble?"

She looked into his eyes, holding his gaze for a long moment before replying. "His aura was tinged with black. I fear something ill may happen to him."

Owst shrugged. "Nothing we can do about it."

Madame Chevellier looked away and said nothing. But she thought, perhaps there is something to be done. She began searching the crowd for Inspector Bradnum.

Livery uniforms seemed to be the ticket that Patrick Sweeney needed to gain access to any location he wished, he thought as he stood in front of the faded glass in the back room of the Waltham Street Hotel. It was a small shabby room, dismally lit, where the waiters dressed before presenting themselves to the upper classes of society that filled the hotel's ballroom. He looked closer at his image and straightened his bow tie so the ends hung in equal lengths. Mustn't call attention to himself in any way.

In the service corridor outside the ballroom, Sweeney queued with the other men waiting to converge on the ballroom with trays of delectables to whet the appetites of those inside. At a signal from the head man, the queue began filing into an anteroom to pick up the trays. Sweeney patted the packet of powders in his trouser pocket and shuffled forward with the rest of the group.

Inside the ballroom, Sweeney made several passes down the right side, always keeping the king and the president in his peripheral vision. He smiled pleasantly at the guests and responded to their questions about the composition of the delicacies he offered on his tray. When the last appetizer had been snatched from his silver tray, he hustled back to the staging area and repeated the sequence. Armed with a freshly-filled tray, he stopped for a moment at the side of the doorway to the ballroom and set down his tray, bending down to adjust his boot lace. As he did so, he pulled the packet of power from his trouser pocket and spread it across the food. The crystals in the packet were practically transparent and were quickly absorbed by the appetizers.

"Get moving over there," the head man shouted.

Keeping his head down, Sweeney waved to him, picked up the tray, and stepped into the ballroom. Several people stepped forward to take items from his tray, but he dissuaded them quickly.

"Special for the king. Special for the president," he said, lowering his gaze to focus on the forest of people in front of him. As he drew near the group around the king and president, he drew a deep breath and pressed forward.

"Your majesty, some caviar, perhaps," Earle said as Sweeney pushed through the crowd.

"Not at the moment," the king said, waving his hand over the tray. "I think I have had enough."

"Mr. President?" Earle had turned to Roosevelt, his hand extended toward Sweeney's tray. Sweeney could feel the sweat begin to bead up on his forehead. He hoped no one would notice it.

Roosevelt puffed his chest out and smiled widely. "Thank you, J. R., but I believe I shall wait for the dinner service." He turned and greeted an elderly dowager wearing a large hat decorated with peacock feathers.

"Well I certainly will try one," said a matron with a diamond bracelet glistening on her wrist. She took one of the appetizers and indelicately stuffed it into her mouth, before quickly reaching forward and taking a second one.

Before he knew it, Sweeney was mobbed by ladies and gentlemen, all intent on getting on of the delicacies that had been offered to the king and president. Within two minutes, the tray was empty.

Sweeney tried to control his breathing as his heart rate accelerated. He had failed, he knew. Neither the king nor the president had taken any of the poisoned food. Within minutes, the guests who had ingested the poison would begin to feel ill. He knew he could not be in the room when that happened.

Sweeney pushed the tray above his head and strode through the room to the doorway to the staging area. He paused there and looked back toward the center of the room, straight into the gaze of Inspector Herbert Bradnum.

Inspector Bradnum, watching the king and president handling the reception's guests, felt a twinge as the waiter pushed his tray of food close to the king. Something about the man made Bradnum look him up and down. The man had sweat on his brow, but who wouldn't in such a close atmosphere, he thought. The waiter turned to Roosevelt, who declined, seemingly to the waiter's annoyance. Bradnum thought he was fairly accurate in reading the unspoken messages on people's faces when they were confronted with unexpected circumstances. This waiter seemed nonplussed when neither the king nor the president took any of the food offered.

Bradnum kept a close eye on the king and president for the next few minutes, and then followed the progress of the waiter as he made his way across the ballroom to the far wall. The man paused at the doorway and looked directly at him. Bradnum knew something was amiss by the look on the waiter's face. He was hiding something.

As the man disappeared through the doorway, Bradnum heard a commotion over by the king. A woman had fainted and was being laid gently on the ground. Bradnum pushed through the crowd that had formed around her and watched as someone produced smelling salts and waved it under her nose. The smelling salts had no effect.

Before he could take a step in the woman's direction, a man to his right collapsed onto the floor, clutching at his collar and breathing heavily. Then another man, an elderly gentleman, collapsed in front of him, causing Bradnum to catch the man to break his fall. As he laid the man on the hardwood floor, a single thought flashed through Bradnum's mind. Poison.

Bradnum bolted for the door the waiter had gone through and crashed through it, knocking down a waiter coming the other way with a tray of food. The two of them went sprawling and bits of the food sprayed across them both. Bradnum got up, and slipping on the slimy floor, ran through the staging room to the exit.

At the far end of the corridor leading to the main staircase he found a hotel porter manhandling a bag up the stairs.

"Did you see a sandy-haired gent coming down the stairs? He would have had a waiter's uniform on."

The porter scratched his head, seemingly grateful for the break. "Aye, he ran past me down there on the landing. He was headed for the front door."

Bradnum raced down the stairs and out into the street. The forecourt was a madhouse of activity. Cabs, carriages and cars were drawn up in front of the building, either discharging passengers or taking them on. Knots of people milled around in front of the hotel, while the pavement out front was crowded with passers-by. The sound of traffic out in the road told him that avenue was full to capacity too.

He pushed his way through the people blocking his progress and found himself a bit of clear space at the junction of the road and the pavement. He first looked south toward Queen Victoria Square, but could see no sign of his quarry. Turning north, he angled left and then right, trying to get a better view of the pavement. Just as he was about to turn again, something caught his eye. It was the gold and black livery pattern of the waistcoat of the Waltham Street Hotel. He had his man in sight.

Bradnum ran up the gutter, splashing in the rivulet of dirty water that trickled there, waving at pedestrians and shouting for them to give way. He had gained on his quarry by half the distance when the man suddenly turned to the right and disappeared. When Bradnum came to the spot where he thought the man had turned, there was nothing but the narrow space between two buildings. At one time, the space might have been a full-sized alley, but both wooden structures had taken to leaning toward each other so that they formed a covered archway now instead of an alley.

Bradnum ducked into the gloom and worked his way along the trash strewn in the alley to a rear yard surrounded by a head-high wooden fence. He was alone. There was no one there. He pulled a dilapidated box over to the fence and peered over it. He could see no sign of the man. He had lost him.

Chapter Sixteen

Inspector Bradnum stepped into the shadow of a thick column at the back of Elmfield House's entry hallway and surveyed what he had accomplished. An armed constable stood at what Bradnum surmised the fellow believed was a ready position, although any newly-named Army corporal would have called the pose lounging. Bradnum thought about strolling over there and reminding the constable of his responsibilities to the king, but then thought better of the idea.

The poisonings at the reception the previous night had given the case an even more bizarre quality that it already had taken. The superintendent had accosted Bradnum early that morning at the station and had torn him apart. Bradnum winced at thought of the superintendent's onion breath washing over his face, the man's mouth just inches from him. The superintendent ranted for a minute or two about the importance of protecting the king and the president, and then launched into a profanity-laced history of what he believed to be Bradnum's intellectual capacity, policing ability and parentage.

Bradnum had borne it all with a straight face, even though he felt the anger boiling up within him. He had wished for some Eno's Fruit Salts at that moment. When the super finished, he had narrowed his eyes. "If anything happens to either of them, even a scratch, I'll nail your bollocks to the wall of my office," he had said. With that threat hanging pregnant in the air, the superintendent had stomped out of the room.

Bradnum shuddered and looked around the room to dispel the thought of speaking in an inordinately high voice. At the corridor entrance from the entry hallway to the main part of the house stood another constable, this one more erect and seemingly concerned about his surroundings. As Bradnum scrutinized the room, he fixed on a large window, its drapes open to the morning light. Outside on the lawn, an Army private paced by carrying a Lee Enfield rifle on his left shoulder.

The inspector smiled. It had been a remark made by the superintendent that had triggered what Bradnum believed was the first mobilization of the British Army for police purposes in the city of Hull. The superintendent had spit out some bit of advice that morning to the effect that he didn't give a rat's arse what Bradnum had to do to protect the king and president, even to the point of calling out the Army. Bradnum had thought it bluster at the time, but after careful reflection, saw the beauty in the superintendent's hyperbole.

Bradnum had the good fortune of being closely acquainted with the colonel who commanded the 15th Foot, the East Yorkshire Regiment. The regiment kept a company of men, more than 125 strong, on the northern fringes of the town and Bradnum had quickly prevailed upon the colonel's love of king and country. By late morning, a platoon of infantry, fully kitted out and armed, had been deployed outside Elmfield House to protect its occupants. The Tommies ran regular patrols throughout the grounds, established sentry positions around the house itself, and manned checkpoints at the roads leading into the estate.

The assistance of the Army allowed Bradnum to deploy the constables under his command throughout the interior of the house. He also had assigned a contingent of his best men to serve as personal bodyguards for the king and president for the duration of their stay in Hull.

Bradnum had spoken with Thomas Taylor, King Edward VII's private secretary, about canceling the tramway rededication, but the man had turned him away. The king would not be cowed by anarchists, he had said. Roosevelt's man, Robert Wallace, had simply smiled and told him that the man who had charged up San Juan Hill wasn't afraid of showing his face at a public ceremony.

Bradnum drew in a deep breath and exhaled loudly. He wasn't a card player, but he knew that the cards he had been dealt on this job were crappy. He had to figure out a way to make them work for him.

&

Madame Chevellier shifted in the plush armchair and watched the houseman approach from the double-door entry to the sitting room.

"The inspector begs your pardon, Madame. He is occupied at the moment, but will join you shortly."

The houseman inclined his head toward her and left. She looked around the room, making comparisons. It is as I saw it in my night dreams, she thought. The sofa table with the long hanging runner over at the side wall. The double thick drapes that could shut out the light entirely when closely drawn. The thick fabric of the chair she now sat in. It is all as I have seen it before, she mused, yet this is my first visit to the house.

The door opening interrupted her thoughts and she watched Inspector Bradnum move across the thick carpet and lower himself into a chair set at right angles to hers.

"Madame Chevellier, it is a pleasure to see you again. I trust this is a matter of some urgency, because as you can imagine, I am quite busy."

Bradnum's face was a mask to her today. Usually he was quite open and readable, but today was different. He must be under considerable stress, she decided.

She opened her eyes wide and smiled at him. "Inspector. I fully realize how the pressures of your job weigh heavily upon you, especially today. But I must tell you of an incident of which I have learned."

Bradnum leaned toward her. "Has someone threatened you?"

She shook her head. "No, it is not me who is in danger. It is the American president, Roosevelt."

Bradnum leaned back and exhaled loudly, as if he had been holding his breath. "You are not telling me anything I do not already know."

Madame Chevellier narrowed her eyes and her lips formed into a tight line. "I had another dream about the president. It was not a good one."

"Madame," Bradnum began. "Have we not gone down this lane before?"

She nodded. "And have I not been proved right with everything I have told you from my dreams?"

Bradnum raised his hand and stroked his chin. "You have been more right than wrong, I will warrant that." He hesitated, still rubbing his fingers under his chin. "Tell me about it," he said, finally.

She closed her eyes and again saw the images from the previous night. "The president and the king are on a raised platform together, somewhere near a street. There are crowds of people around them in the streets, cheering and shouting at the two of them. A band is playing off to the side. I cannot quite make out the tune, but I believe it to be God Save the King."

Madame Chevellier paused and drew a lace handkerchief from the sleeve at her left wrist and daubed at the corner of her mouth with it. She breathed deeply and continued.

"There is a commotion at the back of the crowd, some type of altercation and yet I cannot make out what it is. But it is the type of altercation that bodes no good omen. The king and the president, both standing near some type of machinery that I cannot clearly see, are looking toward the area of the commotion."

She paused again, and then spoke rapidly.

"There is a loud flash and the sound of thunder, but whether it is actual thunder and lightning or something else, I cannot say. I also do not see the sky in my dream, so I do not know what type of weather persists there. When the flash has gone and the smoke clears on the platform, the king is still standing, but the American president is lying on the ground. It does not appear that he is breathing."

Bradnum had inched forward until he was sitting on the edge of his chair. As she finished, he scooted back into the soft cushions and then raised his forefinger to her.

"You are being forthright with me, are you not, woman?"

She held his stony gaze for a long moment. "Aye. That I am. I only tell you what I have seen."

Bradnum stood and looked down at her. "I am trusting you," he said. "God help me if I am wrong."

❧

"This man, Purling," Bradnum said to Glew and another constable, Whiteside, "he has 'trouble' written all over him. I want the two of you to go over to the Tramway Depot and collect this man. Bring him into the station, in manacles if you have to. I want to have a few words with him. He's the buggar that was at the reception last night, trying to get in to see the king and president. Needless to say, he did not have an invitation." Bradnum stopped to stifle a belch with the back of his hand. "J. R. Earle sent the man on his way. I think it is time we had a long, probing conversation with Mr. Purling."

Glew elbowed Whiteside as they left the station, stepping out onto the crowded pavement.

"That inspector is a right rum one, eh, Whitey?"

Whiteside shrugged. "I does what I'm told. He says pick up this Purling bloke, that's what I shall do."

Glew grinned at Whiteside. "How long have you been on the force now?"

"Seven years."

"And you still don't know when you have an opportunity to get on the good side of an inspector who can help you?"

Whiteside only shrugged again.

They engaged a dilapidated open carriage cab at the corner and quickly were clopping along the cobblestones toward a courtyard off 67 Flinton Street, down by the St. Andrew's dock.

"Hold it, cabby," Glew called. "Pull over here."

Glew told the driver to wait, that they would soon return with another passenger. No double the deep blue of his uniform helped make up the driver's mind to comply. Glew led Whiteside down a narrow space between numbers 67 and 68 Flinton Street to a dingy, grimy trash-strewn courtyard at the back of the buildings. At the far side of the courtyard, an open staircase led to the first floor of a weathered wooden building. While Whiteside waited on the ground, Glew ascended the stairs and then pounded on the flimsy door.

He cocked his head as he heard scraping sounds coming from inside the room, and hammered on the door a second time.

"It's the police. Open the door. We want a word with you."

Glew tried the door latch, but it didn't move. The door was bolted. The scraping sounds got louder and Glew hammered a third time. He motioned Whiteside to join him.

"Hull police constables. Let us in or we'll take the door down."

There was no response from inside the room.

"Right, Whitey. On three, we'll bust down the door. One, two, three."

The two constables rammed their shoulders into the flimsy door and crashed it from its hinges, the pair of them sprawling into the room atop the door sliding on the plank floor. Glew regained his feet first. He looked wildly around the shabby room and quickly saw the open window at the back.

Glew pushed his head and shoulders through the window, stretching for a look outside.

"Oh, shit," he said, pulling back inside. "Whitey, let's go. Our man has bolted across the back garden. He's two fences over already and moving fast."

By the time Glew and Whiteside got over the second garden fence they were faced with nothing but gardenias.

Chapter Seventeen

"How the hell could you bloody lose him?" Bradnum shouted. "The man didn't even know you would be there looking for him. How did he give you the slip?"

Bradnum paced up and down a narrow aisle in the cluttered office, turning to face Glew again.

"Well?"

"I have no excuse, sir."

Bradnum stared at Glew for a long moment.

"And why didn't you send Whiteside around to the rear of the building? You had the front bloody well covered yourself."

Glew and Whiteside stood at attention in front of Bradnum's desk, their eyes focused straight ahead and their faces betraying no emotion. Bradnum looked the pair up and down again.

"Get the hell out of my sight."

As the constables each tried to be first through the doorway, Bradnum called out.

"Glew, a moment of your time, if you will."

Glew stopped short and slowly turned to face Bradnum.

"Take a chair, Glew."

Glew moved back into the office as if he were picking his way through a pasture littered with cow dung. He sat in the tattered old chair in front of Bradnum's desk, his gaze following Bradnum as the inspector paced back and forth.

Abruptly Bradnum sat down and slid open a desk drawer, withdrawing a blue bottle that he uncorked and raised to his lips. He wiped his lips with the back of his hand and replaced the bottle in the drawer, slapping it shut with his shin. He looked straight at Glew.

"Dinneford's Magnesia," he said. "It's the only thing that gets rid of this damn indigestion that I get when cases go sour."

Glew nodded, but didn't say anything.

Bradnum, still looking at Glew with a sergeant-major's glare, finally exhaled loudly.

"Relax, Glew. I shan't scream at you again. I want a sympathetic ear."

"Sir? I don't know what you mean."

"Just this. Sit there and listen. If you have a comment on what I say, by all means tell me. I am trying to puzzle out this damned case so that we don't end up with a dead king or a dead American president, or both."

Bradnum saw he had Glew's full attention.

"You have worked with this Purling chap and reported that he is a fine engineer, but a man of limited social skills. Is that correct?"

"Aye, Purling is much more comfortable with machinery than he is with people. He even talks to the machines, almost like..."

"Like what, Glew?"

The constable shrugged. "Like they was his family."

Bradnum pulled at his chin, pinching his lower lip between his fingers.

"And he has no living family that we know of, does he?"

Glen shook his head.

"And Purling certainly has been vocal in his criticism of J. R. Earle and the Hull Tramway Company, has he not?"

"That he has. In fact, the last time I worked with him he told me that Mr. Earle would soon regret the ill treatment that he gave his workers. Purling said he was going to set the balance straight."

Bradnum leaned back and gazed at the ceiling.

"What the devil do you think he meant by setting the balance straight?"

Glew shrugged again. "I suppose that he would somehow take his revenge on Mr. Earle and the tram company."

Bradnum's slowly rose from his chair and his eyes grew wider as he did. He planted his hands on the desk and leaned toward Glew.

"You have done well, Glew."

"I have?"

"Positively. It is so clear to me now. Run out there and have the duty sergeant report to me. I think that we now know where Mr. Purling can be apprehended."

"And where is that?" Glew asked.

Bradnum's face creased into a sly smile. "Why the tram rededication ceremony, of course. It is the one event that he is sure not to miss."

❧

Albert Leake licked the tips of his ink-stained fingers and rubbed them back and forth on his black trousers. No one would know the difference, he thought. Besides, his trouser legs probably carried enough ink on them to print the entire text on the front page of today's *Graphic*, which lay spread on the table in front of him. Leake adjusted a pair of spectacles on the bridge of his nose and leaned closer, reading to himself.

POLICE REMAIN PUZZLED BY RECEPTION POISONINGS

by Albert Leake

Hull police are still devoid of clues that might help identify the villain who poisoned the hors d'oeuvres at the reception given by the American president Roosevelt for King Edward VII at the Waltham Street Hotel on Saturday last.

No motive has been attributed for the dastardly deed, but wisdom suggests that the notable personages at the head of the reception line surely must have been the intended targets of the poison. But to the time of this writing, the police have refused to confirm that either the King or Roosevelt, or perhaps both, were the intended recipients of the poisoned food.

As it developed, some 14 individuals were affected in some way by the poison, believed to be a form of strychnine or rat poison. Eight of those were hurt severely enough to require spending time in hospital, where three of them remain today.

Leake straightened up from the table and pushed his fingers under the spectacles, rubbing his eyes. The damned police had been most unhelpful when he had tried to verify the number and names of the victims of the poisoning. Inspector Bradnum had refused to speak to him at all, while the sergeant who usually doled out information found other duties to attend to rather than talk to him. Leake had finally coaxed some of the information from a constable relatively new to the force, although it had taken plenty of small talk and three cigarettes to accomplish.

Leake pushed the spectacles back down his nose and resumed reading.

> Those still in hospital are Madame Ruth Le Barge, a local dowager who has published two volumes of poetry; Mr. Simon Harris, owner of the coal exporters, modern transport company; and Mrs. Trudy Robbins, wife of the noted solicitor, William Robbins.
>
> The other five individuals who were taken to hospital that night were examined by physicians and released to go home. Six people who ate the poisoned hors d'oeuvres and became ill refused to go to hospital and sought the assistance of their private physicians.
>
> At the heart of the case is the question of not only who would perpetrate such a deed, but why. It must be obvious to the dimmest bulb in the lot that it was not these fourteen people who were the target of the attack, it must have been the King and the American president. And yet the police refuse to speculate on that possibility.
>
> And yet, Hull police have stepped up their efforts at protecting the King and President at J. R. Earle's Elmfield house, even to the point of calling out a platoon of the East Yorkshire regiment to help secure the perimeter of the estate and patrol the grounds.

> It remains to be seen whether the squaddies of the 15th foot will also be used at the rededication ceremonies of the electrification of the Hull Tramway Company lines, where both King Edward VII and President Roosevelt will perform ceremonial duties.

Leake smiled as he read the final paragraph. The idea to suggest in print using the Army at the tram dedication ceremony had leaped upon him like a stag fleeing a hunter and he had hurriedly included the notation, before his better judgment had changed his mind. But was it so fantastic to think that the inspector might not do such a thing? The man had surprised them all in the past, so Leake felt comfortable trying to stay a step ahead.

Leake's problem had been, though, one of a lack of access to information. But he hoped to remedy the situation, at least as far as the other story he was covering — the Tram Man case. Outside the Waltham Street Hotel on the night of the president's reception, he had seen a man ignominiously ejected from the building, so forcefully that the man lost his balance and sprawled onto the pavement. Leake had helped him to his feet and listened as the man ranted about J. R. Earle and the tram company. Leake had pulled a battered pad and a pencil from his pocket and began writing. When the man had drawn a breath, he asked his name.

"Richard Purling," was the reply.

೭

Patrick Sweeney edged closer to the table and spoke in a raspy whisper.

"This bloody project has begun to annoy me. It should not be so difficult to accomplish what we want to do, but we have not succeeded."

William Gallagher sipped a beer while Shamus Loughrey found something or someone of interest across the room to look at. Sweeney saw him looking away.

"If it's not too much bloody trouble, Loughrey, you might want to pay attention to me."

Loughrey snapped his head back in Sweeney' direction.

"Your trouble, Loughrey, is that you're too bloody weak. You don't have the nerve to finish jobs properly."

"That's untrue, Sweeney. I've been a loyal member of the group. You only need to ask and I will do it."

A sly smile crept across Sweeney's face.

"Just ask, eh? That's all I have to do?"

Loughrey gulped hard and nodded.

"Then listen carefully, because I don't want anything to go wrong this time."

Loughrey drew himself up on the stool. "I'm listening, but I'm not hearing anything."

Sweeney narrowed his eyes, but smiled again. "Spunk. That's what I want to see from you. More spunk. Now listen. The president and the king are going to do a ribbon cutting ceremony to mark the anniversary of the electrification of the trams. We are going to be there and are going to use that ceremony to a different kind of dedication."

"What kind of dedication?" Loughrey asked.

Sweeney looked at him like he would at a backward child. "The Cause, you bloody idiot; the Cause."

Loughrey nodded. Next to him, Gallagher had not said a word, but had taken in the entire conversation.

"In order for us to draw attention and support for the cause of Irish freedom, we shall have to involve the Americans. They are lazy and only concerned about what happens on their side of the ocean. We plan on drawing their attention to this side of the Atlantic. We are going to make sure that the Americans rise up on our side against the British."

Gallagher drained his pint mug and asked, "What do you plan to do? Blow up the president?"

Sweeney slowed turned toward Gallagher and a wide smile spread across his face.

"That is exactly what I intend to do."

The words had hardly been out of Sweeney's mouth when Loughrey started breathing heavily and pushed back from the small pub table. He had the look of a stricken deer on his face and his legs trembled. He grabbed the edge of the round table for support.

"I shall not be a part of any killing. Especially, of the... the... President.:"

Loughrey glared at Sweeney, and after casting a sideways look at Gallagher, nodded and left the pub.

Sweeney watched him leave. Once he was through the door, he turned to Gallagher.

"Just like old times in the Republic, eh Boyo? It's just you and me now."

Gallagher took a drink from the fresh pint the barmaid had brought. "You and me," he echoed.

@hapter Eighteen

J.R. Earle had tried to prevail upon the city council to allow him to hold the tram rededication ceremony at a public square near Paragon Station in the center of Hull, but the councilors had balked at the possibility of major city thoroughfares becoming choked by unmovable masses of pedestrian, motorcar, tram and horse carriage traffic. After considerable negotiation and haranguing from Earle, they had allowed the use of Dryport Square and its adjacent green in Hull's eastern ward of Drypool. The square had the advantage of a pair of crossing tram tracks, and it stood only a short distance from the Clarence Corn Mills to the northwest and the Drypool Basin and Victoria Dock to the south.

Inspector Bradnum stood at the head of a wooden barrier erected across Great Union Street where Clarence Street intersected it from the west. He peered toward Dryport Square as a handful of constables moved along behind him, each carrying another section of wood for a new barrier. A wooden platform had been constructed and placed in the blocked section of the road at the Square so that it stood adjacent to the tram tracks that ran down the road's center. When a tram was run up the tracks from the south end of

Great Union Street, it could be brought to a stop adjacent to the platform, where Edward VII and Roosevelt would perform their ceremonial duties.

Bradnum scuffed his boot across the polished tram tracks and then ducked under the barrier, striding down the street. At the front of the platform he turned and faced Drypool Green and studied the raised wooden benches that had been erected on the soft green turf. The entire Green was covered with seating, right up to the row houses that fronted on the Green itself, separated only by a narrow slate walkway. The rear of the Green was bordered by a six-foot-high weathered wooden fence that separated it from the timber yard beyond.

Satisfied that he had the lay of the land of the Green in his mind, he turned back toward the street and almost bumped into Glew, who had quietly crept up behind him.

"Damn, Glew. What the hell are you catting about for?"

"Sorry sir. You said to bring another squad of constables with me." Glew indicated a dozen policemen milling around on the other side of the platform.

Bradnum moved in front of the constables and squared his shoulders.

"Men, you should be aware of how important the security detail for this ceremony is, what with the king and the American president planning to be present. As a precaution, we shall be forced to check the residents of every dwelling along the northeast side of Great Union Street over there, and along the west side of Drypool Green over here." He pointed at the buildings as he spoke and saw each man's gaze follow his pointed direction.

"We need not be concerned about the south exposure, because it is protected by a high wooden fence and there only is a timber yard beyond it. The eastern exposure of the Green, as you can see, is protected by the stone wall that fronts along the graveyard at the side of St. Peter's Church. So we should expect no difficulties from that direction."

A constable at the rear of the group raised his hand. "Beggin' your pardon, sir, but what are we to ask the people in the houses?"

A murmur rose from the group and Bradnum raised his hands for silence.

"We want to be sure that the person or persons who are in residence in each house belong there. You can ask them to provide some kind of proof if you are doubtful about them. If there is any doubt in your mind about a resident, you are instructed to take the individual or individuals into protective custody until the tram rededication ceremony is over and the king and president have left the area."

Another constable piped up. "Sir, what do you mean by questionable?"

Bradnum felt anger rising, but calmed himself. This is no time to shout at a thick constable, he thought.

"Just this, Constable. If you have any doubt at all that the individual you are talking to doesn't belong in the dwelling, then you should remove that person immediately."

"Where shall we take them, sir?"

"We have set up a special area in the Waterloo Public House around the corner to the west on Harcourt Street. Take anyone who is questionable there and make them comfortable in the back room. Constables will be on hand in the pub to be sure no one leaves until the ceremony has finished."

Bradnum looked at the group. "Right. Since you've exhausted your questions, we should get to work. Constable Glew will serve as the coordinator for any individuals removed from their premises. Report to him first, over there at the barrier at the head of the road, before going to the Waterloo. Dismissed, men."

The constables gathered around Glew and he divided them in half, sending the first group along the Green and the second to the other side of the road. When he finished, he turned back to Bradnum.

"Anything else, sir?"

Bradnum put a hand on Glew's shoulder and drew him closer. "This is a very important detail, Glew. We must not mess it up."

"Yes, sir. We won't."

"There are a couple of constables at the barrier up there," Bradnum said, pointing to the blockaded road. "Run up there and have one of them fetch a dozen sets of manacles."

"Manacles, sir?"

Bradnum clapped him on the shoulder and pushed him gently in the direction of the barrier. "Manacles, Glew. We don't know what or who we will encounter in those houses. We should be prepared."

~

The house to house search turned up nothing except a dozen weary constables and a group of uneasy residents of the lower section of Great Union Street. The area wasn't in the league of the posher areas of Hull, but it still served as home to thousands of poorer folks who lived and worked in Drypool Ward's many industries and commercial establishments.

Bradnum had bought a copy of the *Graphic* that morning and read Leake's story about the ceremony, especially noting his mention of calling out the 15th Foot for added protection. But Bradnum was well ahead of the newsman. He had taken a quick lunch at Elmfield House with Colonel Hopkins two days earlier and received the Colonel's guarantee that another platoon of the East Yorkshire Regiment would be made available to patrol the site of the tram rededication ceremony.

Bradnum stood in the middle of the platform and slowly turned in a circle, studying the ground and buildings around the Square and the adjacent Green, the barricades that sealed off the road from traffic, and the placement of constables and soldiers. He drew a deep breath and sighed. He couldn't think of another thing he could do to protect the king and president, short of canceling the entire event, which he had already suggested and been refused.

People had begun to filter into the Square from both ends of Great Union Street, after having undergone scrutiny by constables and soldiers stationed at the barricades at each end of the road.

Bradnum had allowed food vendors to be admitted to the area and to set up on the Green. As long as he controlled the situation, Bradnum reasoned, he may as well make the event as enjoyable as possible for those attending. Each of the vendors had been interviewed by a constable and each cart thoroughly searched for any contraband. None had been found.

Along the west side of the Green were a coffee cart, an eel seller, a fruit cart, a ginger beer and lemonade hawker, and two women with carts selling cakes and tarts. Bradnum's stomach growled as he looked at the food sellers. He had eaten an early breakfast at 5 am of nearly-cold, congealed oatmeal, a poached egg and a crust of stale bread. The breakfast was not carrying him far into the depths of the morning.

Bradnum started down the open staircase at the side of the stage and as he looked out over the crowd a movement caught his eye. Someone had ducked down underneath a set of the raised benches. It appeared to be a man wearing a soft green hat and a tan coat. Bradnum took the stairs two at a time and landed on the roadway harder than he would have wished. He motioned to Glew.

"Come with me, quickly."

The pair wove through the crowd as it snaked its way toward the seating area. As they neared the benches, Bradnum broke off to the right, with Glew following him closely. Bradnum ducked around a coffee seller's cart at the end of the row of benches and peered under the raised end. Crouched there was Richard Purling, wearing a tan coat and green hat.

As Bradnum lurched forward, Purling skittered out of his grasp and hustled in a stooped run under the raised benches to the other end. Bradnum grabbed at him, but came up with nothing but air.

"Glew, get after him."

He had hardly shouted when Glew shouldered past him, running fast after Purling.

Purling exploded out of the far side of the raised benches and headed directly for the fence that separated the Green from the timber yard. He leaped at the six-foot-high fence and pulled himself up so his chest was just above its top. Purling paused to look back at Glew running toward him and just as Glew reached the fence, Purling dropped over onto the other side.

Glew was up to the top of the fence within a moment and flipped over it, sprawling onto the soft dirt on the other side. Purling was laying there next to him, groaning and holding his ankle. Glew pulled a pair of manacles from his jacket pocket and locked them on Purling's wrists.

"I arrest you in the name of the law," he said, and then sat down next to the injured man, breathing heavily.

ॐ

Inspector Bradnum burst into the front office of the bag and sack merchants, A. Kewley and Company, across the road from Clarence Corn Mills, and pulled his warrant card from his pocket, waving it at a pudgy clerk behind a chest-high counter. "The managing director, if you please. Police business."

The clerk's eyes grew wide as he looked past Bradnum toward Glew and two other constables who half dragged Richard Purling through the front door before they unceremoniously dumped him into a wooden chair.

"The managing director," Bradnum insisted.

The clerk shot through an open doorway quicker than Bradnum thought possible and returned with an elderly, pinch-faced man with thinning gray hair.

"What is the meaning of this commotion?" the man asked, standing with his chin thrust forward and his hands on his hips.

Bradnum waved his warrant card at the man and half-turned to indicate Purling. "Inspector Herbert Bradnum of the Hull Police," he said, leaning closer to the managing director. "I am in charge of the security arrangements for the king's appearance at Drypool Square and am in dire need of a private room to interrogate a suspect."

The managing director pulled a white handkerchief from his left cuff and touched his lips before waving it toward Purling.

"Take him away. We have no room such as you require."

Bradnum stared at the managing director for several seconds, and then leaned still closer, his voice a loud whisper.

"If you do not find a quiet room for me to question this suspect, then I shall assume you are hostile to the police and will make it my business to find some obscure city regulation that your business has broken and charge you with the crime." Bradnum straightened up and cocked his head. "What say you now?"

The managing director touched his lips with the handkerchief and then cleared his throat.

"We always have been supportive of the police. I suppose my office would suffice for your purposes."

"Splendid!" Bradnum boomed, clapping the man on his thin shoulder. "Lead the way."

When they had wrestled Purling into the office and put him in a chair in the center of the room, Bradnum dismissed the two constables, but kept Glew with him.

"Take off the manacles and let Mr. Purling recover a bit."

When Glew had removed the manacles, Purling kneaded his wrists where the metal had bitten into the skin. "Don't know why you had to have the damn things on so tight."

Bradnum eased his butt onto the edge of the desk, one leg dangling over the side. "We do so in order that our charges don't consider ill-advised attempts at escape."

A sneer formed on Purling's face and he turned to face Glew. "And you. I taught you things I have not shown anyone else at the depot. I thought I could trust you. But you're a copper, that's plain to see now."

Glew shrugged, but said nothing.

"The constable was acting under my direct orders, Mr. Purling," Bradnum said. "If you have an objection to his actions, you should take it up with me."

Purling glowered at Bradnum, and then shook his head.

"Mr. Purling, we have serious concerns about your presence today at the tram rededication ceremony. Would you please tell us why you are here?"

Purling hunched his shoulders and mumbled.

"I did not hear you. You wanted to see the king, perhaps, Mr. Purling?"

"I care not for the king, nor anyone else."

Bradnum arched his eyebrows. "That cannot be so, Mr. Purling. I have been told that you care greatly for what happens at Hull Tramway Company. You are especially concerned about the behavior of J. R. Earle, are you not?"

"That man," Purling hissed. He drew a deep breath. "Earle has done nothing but pillage the town in the name of business and trample on the rights of good workers in his employ. He lives the life of a country squire, but denies his employees of the basic necessities. He is foul and a stain on society."

Surprised by the outburst, Bradnum decided to continue to prod his suspect. "And as a stain on society, it was necessary for someone to remove that stain, is that right?"

Purling's eyes widened and he nodded quickly. "Yes, yes, of course. You see it now. No one else had the courage to stand up against Earle, so it was left to me. That's why I did it."

"Did what, Mr. Purling?"

"Took him and the company on, of course. It was me who derailed the trams. It was me who assaulted the passengers. It was me who done in that toady, council member Ascot, for doing Earle's bidding. And it was me who set the electrical generation equipment for today's surprise."

A cold chill swept down Bradnum's spine. He chose his words carefully. "Exactly what kind of surprise have you planned, Mr. Purling?"

Purling leaned back in the chair and smiled widely. "J. R. Earle will be on the platform next to the king and the American president to cut the ribbon today. I have set a timing device on the electrical generation equipment that will send a huge bolt of electricity along the lines to the tram used in the rededication. It was a tram that I rigged out myself." He snapped his fingers sharply. "There you have it. An electrical explosion. Too bad for anyone around J. R. Earle."

Bradnum was off the desk and halfway to the door. "Cuff him to that iron pipe over there," he shouted to Glew, "and then follow me. We have to get to the ceremony before the king and the president get on that platform."

≈

Patrick Sweeney walked swiftly along St. Peter's Terrace until he reached its end at the front of a three story brick house that had been divided into a series of flats. Slipping into a narrow alley along the east side of the house, Sweeney emerged into a unkempt, overgrown garden surrounded by a stout wooden fence. After determining that he was alone, Sweeney crossed the open space and pulled himself to the top of the fence, and then dropped onto the other side.

He was now in another back garden, but this one belonged to Number 78 Great Union Street, a three-story structure directly across from the raised platform where the king and president would ceremoniously cut the ribbon. The police had considerately blockaded the road along the pavement in front of Number 78 to allow for space to park the vehicles that the king and the president would arrive in.

Sweeney hefted the satchel he carried and moved to the ground floor rear door of Number 78. It was locked. Looking left and right to be sure he was unseen, he pulled a short piece of iron from his pocket and inserted it above the hasp of the lock in the door. He gave the stout iron bar a quick pull and the sharp cracking sound of wood split the air. Sweeney looked around again, and seeing no movement, stepped through the doorway and pulled the door closed behind him.

The dim interior stairwell smelled of old trash and even older urine. Sweeney carefully picked his way up he stairs to the roof level where he cracked the door open and examined the roof. There was no one there, except for a pigeon coop in the back corner. Sweeney shut the door behind him and duck-walked along the roof so he would not be seen from across the road. When he gained the cover of a chimney at the front part of the roof, he stood up straight for a few moments to get his bearings on the street below. After a quick look he knew it would not be enough and decided he had to get closer.

At the low parapet in the front of Number 78, Sweeney hunched down to avoid silhouetting himself on the roof. Slowly, as he heard a cheer go up from below, he half-stood and surveyed the scene in the Square.

J. R. Earle had just arrived and exited his touring car, which was parked at the edge of the roadway closest to Number 78. Sweeney quickly checked the nearby rooftops to see if constables had been stationed there, but they were empty. In fact, all of the rooftops around him were empty. Apparently the police had prevented the residents from getting on the rooftops for the ceremony. No matter, he thought, it will only benefit the cause.

Sweeney ducked down below the parapet and rustled in the satchel, drawing out four sticks of dynamite, a length of quick fuse and a pocket knife. He cut the quick fuse into equal lengths and pushed each one deeply into a stick of dynamite. He then twisted the fuses together to form a single fuse to be lit.

Pulling two lengths of stout twine from the bag, he wound them around the four sticks of dynamite so they formed a single, solid unit. He set the dynamite aside at the base of the parapet. Then he withdrew a small, shielded lantern with a candle in it from the satchel. He lit the candle and shut the shield, ready to light the fuse when he needed it. This he also set at the base of the parapet, but well away from the dynamite.

Sweeney had initially thought of dropping the dynamite on the president's car when it first stopped below him, but had discarded that idea because too much attention would be on Roosevelt as he arrived for the ceremony. Better to bomb the car when Roosevelt returned to it after the ceremony when the attention of most people would be elsewhere. It would be the safest time for him to drop the dynamite and still escape from the roof. He had no intention of being caught.

Sweeney drew a deep breath and sat cross-legged in front of his equipment. It would not be long now before the American president arrived.

Chapter Nineteen

The driver of the Napier saloon car brought the heavy vehicle to a smooth stop and almost immediately a footman had the rear door open. As King Edward VII rose to exit the car, a loud cheer of "God Save the King" went up from the crowd, followed by extended applause. The king stepped out of the vehicle and nodded toward the crowd before turning toward back toward Roosevelt, who had stood up in the rear of the open touring car. As the crowd roared louder, Roosevelt raised his clasped hands above his head and smiled widely.

"Come, Theodore," the king said. "We must get onto business."

"Yes, of course, Edward. But you shouldn't deny a man his just acclaim. No doubt the people have heard that I have won our wager and are seeking to show their approval." Roosevelt stepped onto the roadway and thrust out his chest, still smiling and waving at the crowd.

A wry smile played across the king's face. "Perhaps they have. Or perhaps they are simply pleased at your appearance with a royal."

Roosevelt cocked his head toward the king. "Don't worry, Edward. I shall be gone in a few days and you'll have them all to yourself once again."

They walked in step toward the platform, where Earle, the mayor and other city dignitaries stood waiting.

"Theodore, you are incorrigible," the king said with a light laugh.

"That's probably one of the nicer things that has been said about me, your majesty."

As they reached the top of the staircase to the platform, Earle stepped forward and bowed to the king. "Welcome, your majesty," he said. Turning to Roosevelt, he offered his hand, which the president clasped. "Mr. President, we are most grateful that you could join us on this happy occasion."

"Pleased to be here, Mr. Earle," Roosevelt responded with a side glance at the king. "Very pleased, indeed."

An attendant led the group to chairs that had been arranged facing the crowd that threatened to overflow the space available on the Green. After the king and president sat down, a commotion arose on the Green to the left of the platform where a half dozen young men had moved forward and began chanting "Long Live Ireland." Three of them unfurled a cloth banner with the same slogan painted in red across its face.

As the chants grew louder and the men moved closer to the platform, constables converged on the Irish protesters and pushed the men back toward the bleachers. Two of the Irishmen threw punches at constables and very quickly the protest turned into a punching melee. More constables poured forward and waded into the fight. With the help of well-placed blows from their truncheons, the constables gained the upper hand and ended the protest by knocking the protestors unconscious.

The crowd, which had cheered wildly at the prospect of additional entertainment, grew silent as constables bundled up the blood-stained banner and dragged the protestors away from the area.

Earle rose and moved to the front of the platform. "Ladies and gentlemen," he said in a loud voice. "We beg your indulgence at the disgraceful conduct you have seen here today. But we shall not let it spoil our ceremony."

As he spoke, the double ringing of a bell sounded from down the street.

Earle smiled at the crowd. "I do believe I hear our tram. We shall begin the ceremony momentarily.

&

Inspector Bradnum raced around the corner onto Great Union Street and skidded into a wooden police barrier at the head of the road, bumping his thigh on a protruding post. He grabbed his leg and rubbed furiously as tears of pain formed in the corners of his eyes. Down the block, the tramway's newest Preston double deck tram, number 57, had glided to a stop alongside the platform. As Bradnum began to limp down the street, still rubbing his thigh as he ran, he saw a pair of tramway employees fasten a wide red ribbon across the side of the tram. He could hear the noise of the crowd now and knew he would have to shout in order to be heard.

"Don't go near the tram," he yelled in breathless bursts.

He ran as fast as his injured leg allowed him, but could plainly see that he would be too late to affect the outcome of the plot that was playing out on the platform. The king and Roosevelt had both stood and moved to the edge of the platform next to the tram.

Bradnum forced himself to run faster, ignoring the pain in his leg.

"Get away from the tram. Get out of there. It will explode."

They still couldn't hear him.

Earle took large pair of shears from an assistant and presented them to the king, handles first. Earle then passed another pair of shears to Roosevelt. As the king and president stood poised to cut the ribbon, Earle raised his hands over his head and asked the crowd for quiet.

As the cacophony of voices died away on the Green, Bradnum stumbled to the side of the platform and shouted, "Get away from the tram. It's rigged to explode. Get off of the platform now!"

Bradnum turned to two constables at the base of the stairway to the platform. "Get them out of here. Bring them to the cars immediately."

While the two policeman mounted the stairs, the king and president moved toward the stairs and met them at the top step.

"What is happening here?" the king asked.

"Orders, your majesty. Please come with us. It's for your safety."

As the constables hustled the king and president toward their cars, Bradnum mounted the steps and called to the rest of the people still milling around on the platform.

"Get off the platform. The tram is set to explode."

Earle, who had stood dumbstruck at the spectacle of the king and president being hustled away from his ceremony, stepped forward with his arms spread wide. "Wait. There's no need to go anywhere. Bradnum, what the devil are you talking about?"

"Mr. Earle, there's no time," Bradnum said, turning to see the king and president being manhandled into their cars.

Out of the corner of his eye, Bradnum saw Glew skidding to a stop near the platform and took a step down toward him as a white-hot flash of electricity exploded at the top of the tram pole. The bolt showered the platform in an umbrella of sparks as the main charge of electrical current coursed down the tram connecting pole and into its driving motor. A split second later, the tram erupted in an explosion of metal and wood pieces that scattered in a wide circle. Earle, the mayor and three councilmen who had been trying to get off the platform were blown off the edge and onto the Green.

Bradnum had been slammed to the ground by the blast. He pushed himself off the soft turf and stood, running his hands over his torso and head, checking for blood. He found none. Glew was beside him in an instant.

"Are you hurt, Inspector?"

"No, I am not, Glew. You?"

Glew shook his head.

"See what you can do to help over there," Bradnum said, cocking his head toward the platform. "I'm going to check on the king and president."

Glew moved toward the remnants of the platform and Bradnum loped across the street toward the two Napier saloon cars. He could see that the black paint on the near sides of both vehicles had been blistered by the explosion's heat and pockmarked by flying debris. He reached for the front door handle of the first car when it suddenly accelerated and sped off down the street.

The second Napier revved its engine and Bradnum stepped in front of the vehicle, holding up his hand. The driver stuck his head out of the open window.

"Where are you taking him?" Bradnum asked.

"Back to Elmfield House."

"I shall meet you there." Bradnum stepped aside and the Napier roared off down Great Union Street.

The sound of humming electricity caused Sweeney's ears to prick up and the hair to stand up on the back of his neck. He got to his knees and peered over the parapet at the tram standing next to the platform when a brilliant ball of electrical fire emerged at the top of the tram connecting pole and exploded in a shower of white-hot sparks. Sweeney involuntarily ducked back down below the top of the parapet and as he did, heard the thunderous explosion of the tram's motor blowing apart. Pieces of metal and wood whizzed over his head and a three-foot slab of the tram's tin roof landed on the roof ten feet away from him.

"By all that's holy, what the bloody hell was that?" Sweeney said aloud.

Slowly he peered over the parapet again. Below him was a scene of confusion and chaos worthy of a Hieronymus Bosch painting. There was nothing left of the tram except the two pair of trucks still standing on the rails cut into the road. The platform looked as if it had been swept by a charred broom. One body lay in its center, unmoving.

Across the Green, people were streaming away from the scene of the explosion, climbing over the fence into the timber yard, pulling themselves over the stone wall into the church's graveyard, and shoving down the alleys between houses lining the Green.

Sweeney saw two policemen hurrying across the street toward the cars below him, each constable with a firm grip on the elbow of the king and the president.

Sweeney snatched up the dynamite and then reached for the shielded lantern. He sagged as he saw what he had done. When the explosion had rocked the street, he had inadvertently kicked over the lantern, extinguishing the flame inside.

He looked back down below him and watched as the first car speed away, and then as the policeman jumped in front of the second one. Sweeney pulled back from the edge of the parapet, but turned an ear toward the sound of the conversation below. Seconds later, Sweeney knew all he needed to know about the destination of the president. He had heard the words, Elmfield House.

I may have missed you here, he thought, but I'll get you before you know it.

Sweeney quickly packed his gear and stepped over the still-smoldering chunk of the tram roof. Attacking at Elmfield House would be tricky, but it was the only card he had left to play.

ॐ

Albert Leake stood at the corner of the stone wall that enclosed St. Peter's Church and its graveyard on the eastern side of the Green furiously writing in his note pad. Streams of people moved past him, some gesturing wildly, all talking in excited tones and in raised voices. The explosion had frightened them badly and excited them at the same time. It had the same effect on Leake, but he forced himself to write a description of the scene as closely as he could remember it.

When he finished his notes, Leake spotted a Napier saloon car speeding away from the square. A second Napier stood across the road and as he watched, Inspector Bradnum stepped in front of the vehicle, preventing it from driving away. He saw Bradnum exchange words with the driver and then step aside to allow the vehicle to follow in the wake of the first car. The saloon cars were the same ones the king and president had arrived in, Leake thought, so no doubt they were returning the pair to Elmfield House. He knew he should follow them, but decided to get a closer look at the damage on the platform first.

The side of the platform facing the Green had received little damage from the explosion, except for the debris on the grass itself. Leake saw the mayor sitting cross-legged on the lawn, holding a red-stained white handkerchief to his bloody forehead. Councilman Abbott lay prone on the ground, breathing heavily as if he were trying to take a deep breath. Councilman Wakefield, his suit blackened by the heat of the blast, wandered in circles repeating, "Where is my hat. I have lost my hat."

Leake hurriedly made notes of what he saw and then ascended the platform steps. In the center of the platform lay a man's body, face down, scorched as if it had been held up to a giant candle. The hair on the back of the head had been burned off by the heat of the explosion. Leake turned the body over and as he released the man's arm, charred bits of the jacket stuck to Leake's hand. Leake wiped his hand down the side of his leg and stared at the lifeless body of J. R. Earle.

છે

After restoring a semblance of order among his constables at the scene of the explosion, Bradnum placed Purling under arrest for murder and directed Glew to clap him in irons and convey him to the station house.

"I shall deal with him shortly. In the meantime, I am going to Elmfield House to check on the king and the president," he said. "Once I am satisfied about their safety, I'll join you at the station and we can take a statement from Mr. Purling about his role in this matter. I don't expect it will be much different than what he has already told us."

At Elmfield House, Bradnum found the security piano-wire taut. He was forced to show his warrant card to two different sentries of the 15th Foot, East Yorkshire Regiment before he was allowed on the premises of the estate. At the main entry to the manor house, two more sentries barred his entry. He hauled out his warrant card again.

Inside in a large sitting room off the entry hall, Bradnum met with Thomas Taylor, the king's private secretary, and

Robert Wallace, Roosevelt's chief of staff. After a half hour reviewing the security arrangements with the two of them, Bradnum felt comfortable enough to leave.

Dusk was settling on the town and the last streaks of sunset were fading when Bradnum finally returned to the main station house. The first person he bumped into was Glew.

"Sir, I think you will want to talk to someone we have over there," Glew said, drawing Bradnum to one side and flicking his gaze toward a dead-eyed Irishman sitting on a wooden bench next to a burly constable. "He says he has some information about the man we're looking for. The man who is trying to harm the king and the president."

Bradnum arched his eyebrows. "Does he, now? Well, bring him into my office and we shall have a chat. I'd like you there too, Glew."

When they had assembled in the office, Bradnum dismissed the burly constable and shut the office door.

"Your name, please?"

The dead-fish eyes stared at Bradnum for a long moment. "Loughrey. Shamus Loughrey."

"Well, Mr. Loughrey, perhaps you'd be so kind as to tell us what is on your mind."

Loughrey opened his mouth to speak, but said nothing. He looked down at the wood plank floor instead.

"Here now, this is no time to get shy, Mr. Loughrey. Do you have information for us or not?"

Loughrey's head snapped up quickly. "I bloody well do," he hissed. "But I shall be putting me own life in jeopardy by the telling of it to you."

Bradnum leaned forward across his desk, his face neutral. "We can protect you."

"Not from these animals and certainly not from Sweeney."

"What animals are those and who might this Mr. Sweeney be?" Bradnum glanced at Glew and saw he already was making notes.

"Patrick Sweeney's the one that will get the president, mark me."

Bradnum leaned back in his chair. "Get him?"

"To be sure," Loughrey said. "Kill him to involve the United States in the Irish cause. It's all that he and Gallagher talk about."

Bradnum exhaled a long breath that sounded like air whooshing down a narrow alley.

"Gallagher?"

"Aye, William Gallagher."

"How does Mr. Sweeney plan to go about this assassination?"

"Well he's missed his chance a few times already. There was the railway siding bombing, and when that failed, the poisonings at the Waltham Street Hotel." Loughrey paused. "And I hear that he did not succeed with the bombing today at the tram ceremony either."

"We do not believe that the explosion at the square was the work of Mr. Sweeney," Bradnum said, leaning forward again. "In fact, we have incontrovertible evidence it was the work of another individual."

Loughrey shrugged. "That simply means Sweeney didn't get the chance to do what he had planned. Someone beat him to it." Loughrey cocked his head and took a long look at Glew and then turned back to hold Bradnum's gaze. "It also means he is not through. He will try again. And this man is so ruthless, I have no doubt he will succeed."

"Well, it is my job to see that he does not. Can you tell me where to find Mr. Sweeney?"

Loughrey nodded haltingly. "I usually met Sweeney at pubs or in parks, so I was never at his place. But Gallagher told me Sweeney often stayed in a small room at the back of the Flying Fish Public House on Roper Street near the Prince's Dock.

Bradnum bit his lower lip and stood. "Mr. Loughrey, you will be our guest here for a while."

After Bradnum summoned the burly constable and Loughrey was manacled and removed from the office, he turned to Glew.

"Let's pay a visit to the Flying Fish. And Glew, bring a revolver."

Chapter Twenty

The Flying Fish Public House stood at the intersection of Roper and Myton Streets, a long block away from a row of warehouses that lined the west side of Prince's Dock along Waterhouse Lane. Half a block down Roper, a tight knot of schoolboys stood on the pavement at the base of the stairs to the Hull Boys Club, listening to their guide lecture them about some point of expected behavior. From the other direction, south along Myton Street, came the sound of metal being tossed into huge bins at the Alexander Copper and Brass Works. The noise from the Works boomed along the street like a fog steadily rolling in from the sea.

Approaching the pub from the west side of Myton Street, Bradnum held his hand up to halt the column of constables accompanying him. He peered at the entrance to the Flying Fish, trying to see inside the pub's open doorway. A thin stream of stale tobacco smoke wafted from the top of the doorway, but Bradnum could see nothing inside except the legs of an empty wooden table.

"Sergeant, you and Bowley nip down the street and pop into the pub's rear yard," Bradnum said. "I expect there may be a door at the back that has access to the rear rooms. If so,

I want that escape route covered. We shall enter from the room's interior. You have your revolver?"

"Aye, sir."

"Then off with you." Bradnum turned to Glew as the two constables hustled down the street. "I expect that it will be quite tight at the rear of the pub. I've never seen back rooms that were spacious. I want to be sure you're prepared to do your duty if needed." He glanced at the Webley revolver tucked into Glew's wide belt.

Glew patted the Webley's butt. "I'm a crack shot, sir. He'll not escape."

"I want him alive, Glew. If that is possible, of course." Bradnum craned his neck and squinted down Roper Street. "It appears the others are in the rear yard. Let's go."

The main barroom of the Flying Fish Public House was crowded with midday drinkers, most of them workmen from the copper and brass works or warehousemen from around the docks. No one paid any attention to Bradnum and Glew as they made their way through the room to the back of the house.

Bradnum stopped in front of a black-painted pine door. "In there, I expect. Are you ready?"

Glew nodded and withdrew the Webley from his belt. There was a loud click as he cocked the hammer.

Bradnum reached down and tightened his grip on the door latch, careful not to make a sound by rattling it. He turned it slowly and leaned his shoulder against the wood. The door opened freely into the room with a soft whoosh of air.

Bradnum stepped through the doorway with his hands high in front of his face, ready for a fight. Glew came on just behind him, pointing the revolver into the room.

As Bradnum's eyes adjusted to the dim light, he looked around the room wildly. The place was empty. Sweeney wasn't there.

&

Sweeney leaned back in the wooden chair and pulled aside the window curtain in the main barroom of the Flying Fish to stare out onto Myton Street. He quickly released the curtain and sat up straight. Two constables were hurrying up the street, seemingly intent on approaching someone in a furtive manner. The big constable had a revolver tucked into his belt.

Sweeney swallowed the last of his beer. Damn fools, he thought. They'll have to be more clever than that to get me. If two constables were headed around to the back of the building, he reasoned there must be at least a couple more coming in the front. He hurried back to his room, snatched up the satchel with his gear and grabbed his coat. He quickly looked around the room. Nothing left for them.

At the end of the corridor, near the door to the water closet, he mounted a narrow staircase to the upper floor. No time to be quiet, he thought as he pounded up the stairs. Only time to be gone. The head of the stairs opened onto a small sitting area off of which there were three doorways. Sweeney ignored the other rooms and went to the window at the far end of the sitting area.

Opening the window carefully, he stuck his head out and checked the flat roof of the back of the next-door building that abutted the public house. It was empty. He pulled on his coat and then dropped the satchel onto the roof, jumping out after it. Reaching up to the open window, he pulled it shut. Sweeney then grabbed the satchel and sprinted across the roof to a second flat roof, and then to an unlatched window on the upper floor of the Boys Club. He was inside within a minute and headed down the stairs toward the entrance on Roper Street.

Out on the street, he turned east and walked quickly to Warehouse Lane where he offered a lumber lorry driver two shillings for a ride to the center of the city. As he pulled himself onto the board seat next to the driver, Sweeney looked back the way he had come and smiled.

❧

Bradnum had hardly dropped into his office chair at the station when a constable appeared in the doorway.

"Beggin' your pardon, sir, but there's a strange woman out here who insists on speakin' with you."

Bradnum let his chin drop to his chest and exhaled a long breath. "Would her name be Madame Chevellier?"

The constable's eyes grew wider. "Bleedin' hell, sir. That's it exactly. I mean, excuse me language sir, but..."

"Not to worry. Just show the woman in."

Madame Chevellier was clothed in her usual costume of a long billowing dress and a colorful head scarf around her hair. Bradnum looked at the rings on her fingers and thought that the weight of so much jewelry might actually prevent her from raising her hands too high.

"Inspector, you don't look very well. Are you ill?"

Bradnum shook his head. "Only a long, tiring day with little to show for a considerable amount of effort. Please excuse me for a moment." He pulled a bottle of Dinneford's Magnesia from a desk drawer and raised the bottle to his lips, taking three large gulps. "My apologies, but this is one of the only remedies that seems to work for me."

Madame Chevellier seemed to be inspecting him closely. "Perhaps you should have a break from your work. A holiday might put you back in proper form."

"A holiday! Now that's a luxury I cannot afford at the moment." Bradnum leaned forward. "How may I help you today?"

"It is I who is here to help you, Inspector. I have had another vision. Last night."

Bradnum waited for her to continue, but she sat there stone faced.

"And? Is there anything else?"

Madame Chevellier drew a deep breath. "The man you are seeking is exceptionally dangerous. He plans to hurt the American president. And he is an Irishman."

Bradnum's gaze had wandered to a report on the desk, but he snapped his attention back to the psychic at the mention of the Irishman. "How do you know he is Irish? Do you know his name?"

She shook her head. "Not his name. But I heard his accent. He is Irish. That I know."

"From your dream. That is where you heard him?"

Madame Chevellier stiffened. "I do not like your tone, Inspector. We have been over this ground before. The visions come to me in my dreams. Have I led you astray thus far?"

Bradnum stood and rubbed his hands. "I intend no disrespect, Madame. But you must realize that police work and visions do not handily go together when one is conducting an investigation."

"I understand."

She began to stand, but changed her mind and sat back down. "There is more."

Bradnum rubbed his eyes. "What would that be?"

"I saw the Irishman slipping into a large estate house. Where it was, I do not know, but it was certainly a grand place."

Bradnum gave her his full attention. "And... ?"

She drew a deep breath and exhaled. "He was lighting something that looked like a fuse. I assume it was attached to explosives."

Bradnum slapped the desktop with a loud smack. "Of course. A bomb at Elmfield House. That is the way he would do it. It seems to be the way he operates."

He glanced at Madame Chevellier, who wore a startled look on her face. "Madame," he said. "You just may have saved the day, and the American president at that."

&

Patrick Sweeney stepped from the bushes at the side of the road and tugged down on the narrow bill of the dirty cap he wore. The work pants chafed against his legs, still stiff from a hard soak and washing in the laundress's place next to the carpenter's shop where he had stolen the clothes. He looked back over his shoulder, and seeing no one else on the street, grabbed the handle on the wooden box of tools sitting at the base of the bushes.

He put a jaunty swagger into his step when the gatehouse that blocked the access to Elmfield House came into view, and started whistling a noisy song slightly out of tune. Sweeney turned into the wide gravel roadway when a sentry, cradling a Long Lee Enfield rifle in his arms, stepped in front of him. Sweeney squinted at the soldier as he approached. The man wore the battle dress of the 15th Foot, the East Yorkshire Regiment.

"Halt. What your business here?"

Sweeney could see a second sentry standing alongside the stone pillar that supported one end of the massive iron-barred gate. The soldier had his finger inside the trigger guard of his rifle.

The two-story high gatehouse formed a deep archway over the roadway, and was formed in a U-shape. Down each wing of the gatehouse, Sweeney could see a series of doors that led to interior rooms. The second floor of the gatehouse had leaded-glass windows at the front and down both wings.

Sweeney cleared his throat and spit onto the side of the roadway. "Hello, Mate. I'm here about the carpentry work." He rattled the tool box and smiled.

"No carpentry work's going on here. Be off with you." The sentry gestured with his chin back toward the main road.

"Here, now. They sent a man to my shop and told me to come along today and repair the damage on the second floor of the gatehouse. Something about a leak in the roof that caused problems with one of the ceilings at the back of the place. I expect they don't want it to fall in."

The sentry looked back at his partner. "Willie, do you know anything about this?"

The second sentry shook his head.

Sweeney saw the situation slipping away and decided to play his final card. He reached into his pocket for the crumpled piece of paper that he had filled out a couple of hours previously. "Hold on. Have a look at this work order. It says what is to be done."

Sweeney held out the paper to the sentry, who took it by a corner as if it were contaminated by lice. Sweeney watched as the sentry's eyes moved back and forth, struggling with the words. The sentry handed the work order back to Sweeney.

"You can come back another day."

Sweeney dropped his toolbox onto the gravel. He shrugged and stuffed the work order into his coveralls pocket. "Mr. Earle will be mighty displeased when he learns you sent me away. He's the one who ordered the work done."

The sentry had stiffened at the mention of Earle's name. Sweeney knew he had to push him over the edge.

"Come on, Mate. It's only the gatehouse. Let me get the work done and then I can get paid by Mr. Earle. You wouldn't begrudge another workingman his daily wage, would you."

The sentry stood immobile for a few more seconds. Then he clucked his tongue and turned to his partner. "Willie, let the bloke through. He's only going into the gatehouse."

The sentry turned back to Sweeney. "Second floor, you said. Right?"

"That's it, exactly."

"Use the second door on the left. Staircase is just inside."

Sweeney put on his brightest smile. "Thanks, Matey. I'll return the favor someday."

The second sentry swung the heavy iron gate open and Sweeney walked under the archway and through the second doorway on the left, closing the door securely behind him. He trudged up the stairs, making sure his heavy boots made as much noise on the wooden planks as he could. When he reached the top, he found a large room at the back of the west wing and dropped the tool box onto the floor, rattling the tools loudly.

Then he quietly moved back down the corridor that ran the length of the wing and peeked out a window overlooking the front of the gatehouse. The two sentries were directly below him, talking quietly. The sentry who had challenged him said something and the pair laughed loudly before they separated and went back to their posts.

Sweeney saw his chance. He returned to the back room, retrieved the tool box, and then quietly made his way down the stairs. There he silently moved down a narrow corridor to a door at the end of the wing at its farthest point from the gate. He drew in a deep breath, opened the door and stepped outside.

There was no one around. To his right was the gravel roadway leading to Elmfield House. To his left was a manicured lawn dotted with boxwood and hibiscus bushes. Sweeney checked behind him and then started off at a fast walk toward the foliage that lined the side of the estate.

⊕

Chapter Twenty-one

Inspector Bradnum wasn't comfortable with riding in a vehicle being driven by Constable Glew, but at least the trip out to Elmfield House gave him a chance to formulate a plan to deal with Sweeney. Bradnum had not understood how the Irishman could stay one step ahead of him and continue to threaten the president. At least that part of the mystery was clear now. Loughrey confirmed that Sweeney wanted to harm President Roosevelt to attract attention in America for the Irish cause. Damn fools, Bradnum thought, smacking the leather seat with a loud slap.

Glew glanced over at him. "Something you wanted, sir?"

Bradnum shook his head. "No, Glew. Just thinking out loud and getting upset about the results."

Out of the corner of his eye Bradnum saw a small smile creep across Glew's face. The young constable was turning into a fine police officer. He was sharp-witted, followed orders implicitly, and seemed to have a knack for being in the proper place at the right time. Bradnum wished he had an entire squad of constables like Glew.

Glew turned off the main road and braked the small vehicle to a jolting halt in front of the massive gatehouse to

Elmfield House. A sentry from the 15th Foot came to attention and saluted, then approached the side of the car.

"Good day, Inspector. Shall we open up for you?"

"Very good, corporal. How are things going here? Anything to report?"

"No, sir. It's been quiet out here, even with the carpenter at work inside the gatehouse."

Bradnum leaned across the gear lever toward the driver's window. "The carpenter, you say? What carpenter?"

The sentry brightened. "The one who's fixing the ceiling up on the first floor. He had the proper work order and Mr. Earle's permission to do the work."

Bradnum leaned back to the passenger side window and cocked an ear. "I don't hear any hammering. Actually, there's no sound of work at all. I think you better get that gate open."

The sentry called to his partner to open the gate and once they were through, Bradnum bolted for the doorway.

"He went up there," the sentry said, pointing up the stairs.

"Glew, stay here. Corporal, come with me." Bradnum pointed to the sentry's rifle. "And chamber a round in that thing."

The wooden planks creaked under his weight as Bradnum creeped up the staircase. The sentry seemed to be better at making less noise than he was. At the top of the stairs Bradnum stepped aside and let the sentry lead the way into the back room that overlooked the lawn at the front of Elmfield House. The room was empty and showed no sign of any carpenter or carpentry work.

"Bloody hell."

Back under the archway, Bradnum met Glew, standing beside the police vehicle.

"He's here," Bradnum said, looking behind him at Elmfield House.

"Who is?" Glew asked.

Bradnum bit his lower lip before answering. "The Irish assassin, Sweeney."

❧

Sweeney slipped from behind spreading boxwoods and strolled toward the workmen's entrance at the rear of Elmfield House as if he hadn't a care in the world. The constable posted at the door was a young fellow, certainly not long on the force, Sweeney thought.

"Your business here, please?" the constable asked, standing ramrod straight in front of the door.

Sweeney set his tool box down and fished the work order from his coveralls pocket. He held it out to the constable. "It's all in there, Matey. They want the water closet fixed."

The constable scanned the crumpled paper and handed it back. "It doesn't say anything about a water closet there." He stood his ground.

"Of course, Matey. The upper class, they don't write about such things as water closets that need to be unstoppered. They just call on me and tell me to get it done. That's what they want."

The constable looked hesitant, but still didn't move aside.

Sweeney shrugged and picked up his tool box. "I suppose you'll be the one to tell Mr. Earle that his water closet will stay full of shit because I wasn't allowed to unstop it." He began to walk away.

"Wait."

Sweeney turned. "What's it going to be, Mate? Yes, or no?"

The young constable stood aside and pushed open the door. "Go on in and get it done. Quickly, mind you."

"You're a right proper mate," Sweeney said with a smile. He quickly went through the doorway and found himself in a tile-floored room. Two walls were taken up by a line of clothes hooks, from which hung an assortment of coats, jackets and shirts. A line of boots and muddy shoes stood along the wall under the clothes.

Sweeney looked down a short corridor and saw a kitchen on the left and a pantry to the right. He sprinted along the corridor and peeked into the pantry before ducking inside.

The room was spacious for a pantry, with shelving and cabinets lining the walls, each crammed from floor to ceiling with glassware, china, cups and saucers, cutlery, non-perishable foodstuffs and linens. A pair of oak pocket doors stood three-quarters open. Beyond them was the dining room.

Sweeney slowly peeked into the dining room and finding it empty, stepped inside. The room was fashioned as a long rectangle, with an oak table seating twelve in the center of the room beneath two crystal chandeliers. Along the wall to the pantry were two large sideboards, each with closed cabinets making up their lower portions.

Sweeney set the tool box down next to the sideboard that stood closest to the head of the table. He rummaged around under the tools until his hands found the burlap-wrapped packages, which he removed and set on the floor.

Unwrapping the first one, he extracted six sticks of dynamite that he had tied tightly together. Fuses protruded from each stick and then were twisted together to form a single, thick length of fuse about four inches long.

From the second burlap package Sweeney withdrew a tight coil of quick fuse, so called because it was the fastest burning type of flame ignition available to detonate dynamite. He unwrapped the end of the fuse and uncoiled several feet to allow himself freedom to work. Quickly he twisted the end of the quick fuse onto the pigtail fuse leading to the dynamite.

Reaching around behind the sideboard, Sweeney slid the fused explosives behind the back wooden panel and placed it on the floor at the base of the wall. When the dynamite detonated, the explosion would be directed out from the stone wall, splintering the wooden sideboard and exploding it into hundreds of lethal splinters that would blow through the dining room and kill its occupants.

Sweeney pushed the fuse cord down into the joint where the floor and the wall met, and then led it around the edge of the doorway and into the pantry. There, he ran the fuse along the base of the cabinets and around the back of the room to the pantry doorway to the corridor.

He returned to the dining room and retrieved his tool box, hiding among the pantry's linens in a lower cabinet. He then laid out the rest of the fuse down the corridor, behind the boots and shoes in the entry hallway. Sweeney set the free end of the quick fuse next to a box of matches behind a pair of Wellington boots and returned to the pantry to wait.

Glew drove up the roadway to the roundabout in front of Elmfield House and before the car before had come to a halt Bradnum had the door open and stepped out. He stumbled in the soft gravel and nearly fell, but recovered his balance and lumbered toward the front door. The constable at that post stiffened to attention.

"Constable. I want this entry sealed. No one comes or goes through that door without my permission. Is that understood?"

"Perfectly, sir."

"Glew, come with me."

Bradnum burst into the entry hallway, startling two constables who stood idly talking to each other.

"Men, we have a situation on our hands. I believe that an assassin has gained access to the grounds of Elmfield House.

He may even be in the house itself. I want one of you to go with constable Glew to search the first floor. The other with accompany me on a search of the ground floor. Now let's get on with it."

Glew and one constable quickly mounted the wide staircase leading from the side of the entry hallway to the first floor. They disappeared into the nearest room off the upstairs corridor.

"Come with me," Bradnum said, motioning the constable forward. "Do you have a weapon?"

"I have me truncheon." The constable pulled the stout wooden stick from his belt and wiggled it.

"Excellent. You may need to use it, so keep it handy. This man we're dealing with has killed before. You can be sure he will not have any compunction about doing so again."

Bradnum moved into the sitting room off the entry hallway, peering behind sofas and chairs, and pushing the window drapes aside to be sure they didn't hide anyone. He and the constable slowly searched all the rooms in the front of the house, but found nothing.

In the kitchen, he found a cook and her helper hard at work, tending a large pot boiling on the wood stove. Across the room, heat shimmered from an oven where chickens were roasting.

"Have you seen any workmen back here today. A carpenter, perhaps."

"Nay, there's been no one but the two of us," the cook replied. "And you two."

"Where does that corridor outside lead?"

"Just the pantry across there and then the back of the house where the servants and workmen come and go."

"Constable, check the pantry. I'll have a look at the back entry."

Bradnum moved down the corridor slowly, trying to keep his weight on the balls of his feet in case he needed to move quickly. Ahead he could see part of the rear entry room with its muddy boots and shoes lining a wall. Coats and jackets hung from pegs nailed to the wall. Bradnum looked around the room. Nowhere to hide in here.

He pulled open the back door and startled the soldier standing there, guarding the entry.

"Carry on," he said, and shut the door firmly. As he moved down the corridor toward the front of the house, the other constable came out of the pantry.

"Anything?" Bradnum asked.

"Not a thing."

Bradnum puffed out his cheeks in a stream of breath. "Damn him. He must be outside yet. Let's get back to the front of the house."

∾

Sweeney leaned against a cabinet and toyed with the idea of reconnoitering the rest of the ground floor when he heard voices coming from the front of the house. He moved to the pantry doorway with the corridor and listened intently. Someone was giving orders to search the house. He looked around the room. The place was packed with goods. The only space where he could fit was a tall closet that held stacks of linens.

Sweeney opened the cabinet door and pulled the linens forward. He then picked up the top third of the stack, stepped in behind the linens, pulled the door shut and set the table linens down hiding himself from view if the door were opened.

He tried to calm himself and slow his breathing so he wouldn't be detected. After two minutes he was calm enough to believe he actually might get away with his ruse. Suddenly he heard the scrape of a boot on the stone floor. He heard voices talking in the kitchen across the hall, and then movement toward him. He held his breath.

He could hear someone moving around in the pantry, poking into cabinets, opening and closing doors. Sweeney tensed his body to spring out if he were discovered. The sounds got closer and then light flooded into the cabinet as the cabinet door was opened. Almost as quickly, the door slammed shut and the light disappeared. Whoever was out there hadn't looked very hard.

Chapter Twenty-two

King Edward VII thrust his shoulders back and strode through the doorway into the brightly-lit dining room. He nodded to Lord Carrington and Roosevelt, and then quickly swiveled toward Lord Roseberry who stood at the far end of the long table.

"Michael, you should move closer down this way toward the three of us. You wouldn't want to be eating by yourself."

Lord Roseberry bowed and plucked at his graying moustache. "I was waiting to see where you would place us, your majesty. And the president was in a close conversation with Lord Carrington..."

Roosevelt snapped his head in Roseberry's direction. "Nothing you couldn't take part in, Michael. Please join us."

Lord Roseberry took a seat opposite Roosevelt and Lord Carrington, facing the sideboard closest to the head of the table, where the king had sat.

The king rang a silver bell and a butler appeared from a side door.

"Clarence, pour us some of that nice claret you have uncorked. I think we all could stand a bit of the grape at this point."

The butler poured the wine and then left, being replaced by two young kitchen maids who served the soup course. When they finished ladling out the thick broth, the king raised his wineglass.

"Gentlemen. To our good friend Theodore, who has graciously put up with the unpleasantness that we have all faced these past days. May you continue in good health, Theodore."

The two lords chimed in with "to your health" before each took a liberal swallow of wine.

"Easy men," the king chided. "There's plenty left in the bottle and an entire cellar full to back it up. No need to be hasty with good wine."

Lord Roseberry's face reddened from ear to ear so that it almost glowed. He lowered his head and concentrated on his soup.

"Your majesty, we are simply trying to keep up with the royal appetite for the finer things in life," Lord Carrington said, raising his glass toward the king. "To your health."

The foursome drank again. Roosevelt was the one to break the ensuing silence.

"Does anyone else smell something burning?" he asked.

আ

Sweeney reached across the darkness and edged the cabinet door open. He could see part of the doorway and it was empty. No sound came from the interior of the pantry so he unfolded himself from his cramped position and pushed the top of the linen stack out onto the floor. Once extricated from the cabinet, he gathered the linens and stowed them in the cabinet, closing the door with a quiet thud.

A voice in the kitchen said something about a sirloin, but Sweeney couldn't hear clearly enough to make sense of what was said. He did know, however, that the sounds of the serving girls moving in and out of the kitchen meant that the dining room was occupied and dinner was being served. Now was the time for him to act.

Peering around the edge of the doorframe, Sweeney checked the hallway. Empty. He slipped along the plaster wall and emerged in the entry room leading to the back door. At the end of the line of shoots and boots, he pushed the Wellingtons aside and snatched up the box of matches. When the first one he struck caught fire, he put the burning tip against the fuse nestled in the joint between the floor and wall. The quick fuse sputtered and then caught, it's flame racing along the wall behind the line of boots and toward the dining room.

Sweeney's eyes glowed as brightly as the quick fuse as he watched it flame and disintegrate as it burned. Time to be gone, he thought. He picked up his toolbox and opened the back door, touching his cap in salute to the constable standing there.

"Pleasant day to you, Mate."

The constable wrinkled his nose and watched as Sweeney disappeared around the corner of the house.

❧

"Damn, we must be missing something," Bradnum said. "Sweeney wouldn't risk showing up here unless he had some unpleasant business planned."

"What could he do here?" Glew asked. "The king and president are secure in the house having dinner. He can't get to them."

Bradnum had turned away from the front of Elmfield House and taken a couple of steps toward the gatehouse when he abruptly stopped.

"Of course," he said. "The dining room. Glew you're a genius."

He ran past Glew up the front steps and stopped in the doorway, looking over his shoulder. "Let's go, Glew. He must be in the house."

Bradnum disappeared into the entry hall and raced down a side corridor toward the rear of the house. The corridor led to a cross hallway between the conservatory and the kitchen. Bradnum bounced off the intersecting wall and stumbled several steps along the hallway until he emerged in the back entry room.

The smell of burning powder was overpowering.

Four steps into the corridor to the dining room, Bradnum could see a sputtering flame running along the base of the wall. It was moving directly toward the dining room.

He ducked down at the flaming end of the fuse and tried to extinguish the flame, but the sparks burnt his hand and he jerked it away. As the flaming end of the fuse disappeared around the corner, Bradnum crashed into the door and burst through the doorway.

He saw the fuse leading to the sideboard and leaped headlong onto the carpeted floor smashing into the sideboard's oak base. As the fuse burned hotly along the base of the wall two feet from the sideboard, he thrust his hand behind the heavy oak, squeezing his arm down toward the floor. He felt his fingers touch a bundle of long hard tubes and then they found the braided cord of the fuse. He tightened his grip and yanked the fuse cord from the dynamite just as the glowing end reached his hand and burned him a second time.

Bradnum, his eyes screwed tightly shut, lay on his back panting.

"I say, Bradnum. What the devil are you doing down there?" the king asked.

Four pairs of eyes were riveted on him. Bradnum reached behind the sideboard and pulled out the wrapped six sticks of dynamite. He stood and thrust the dynamite into his jacket's side pocket, and then dusted himself off. "Just a bit of housekeeping, your majesty. I would like the four of you to remain in this room for the moment. The man who left this calling card is still nearby. It's time for me to have a chat with him."

Chapter Twenty-three

Bradnum barreled down the corridor past the kitchen and pushed through the doorway to the rear yard of Elmfield House, bumping into the young constable guarding the entryway and knocking both of them to the ground.

"Damn, man, get off of me," Bradnum sputtered. "Can't you see he's going to get away?"

"Who is, sir?" the constable asked as he helped Bradnum to his feet.

"The Irish assassin. He's dressed as a workman and probably carrying a box of tools."

A look of astonishment crossed the constable's face. "A man like that came out of the house a few minutes ago. He went that way." The constable pointed toward the side of the house.

"Come with me, man."

They raced to the side of the house and halted near a thick stand of boxwood.

"Check those bushes," Bradnum ordered.

The constable disappeared behind the tall, dense boxwood bushes and reappeared seconds later. "Nothing, sir."

Bradnum squinted toward the front of Elmfield House and could see all the way to the gatehouse where two sentries stood looking back at him.

"Well, he's not gone toward the front, so the only way left is over there." Bradnum pointed to a thick copse of trees on the west side of the Elmfield House estate. "He's got to be in there. Get over to the trees quickly and see if you can spot him. I'm going to get reinforcements started and will be right behind you. And constable, be careful. This man is dangerous."

As the constable double-timed across the lawn toward the trees, Bradnum sprinted around the front of the house where he found a constable and a sentry from the 15th Foot.

"You two, come with me. It's urgent. We have the assassin trapped in the woods." He paused to catch his breath and looked at the sentry. "Soldier, make sure you have a full magazine and one in the chamber. Safety on. Constable, the sentry will lead us into the woods. Now follow me."

Bradnum turned and began running toward the tree line, but quickly found himself falling farther and farther behind the two younger and fitter men. He was only half-way across the wide expanse of lawn when the other two reached the tree line and split up, taking different paths into the woods. The constable angled to the south and the sentry to the north.

Bradnum arrived at the wood's edge wheezing so heavily that he bent over and jammed his hands on his knees, trying to catch his breath. Between gasps, he looked into the thick woods, but could see nothing moving.

Damn, he thought. Where are the three men who went in there after Sweeney?

☙

Once he had cleared the side of Elmfield House, Sweeney set off at a fast walk on a diagonal across the lawn and toward the trees. From the gatehouse, it would appear that he was headed toward one of the outbuildings on that side of the estate. Once safely inside the cover of the tree line, Sweeney ditched the tool box and stripped off the coveralls. He placed them in a small depression and broke off several branches from a leafy bush to camouflage them.

Looking back the way he had come, Sweeney saw a slim constable running across the lawn toward him.

Bejesus, he thought. The bloody English don't give up. Well, I'll give the youngster a surprise.

Sweeney sprinted deeper into the woods, checking over his shoulder as he ran. The constable reached the cover of the tree line just as Sweeney splashed through a narrow brook that took him by surprise. He clambered up the steep bank on its far side and turned to look back. Too late. The constable saw him and began running again.

Sweeney turned and dodged behind an old elm felled by the wind, its branches still covered with now-brown leaves. He looked around for some kind of weapon, discarding the idea of stones and settling on a stout three-foot-long branch. He crouched behind the elm's trunk and waited.

Within minutes he heard the heavy tread of the constable coming toward him. It sounded as if the constable would pass right by his hiding spot. Sweeney raised the heavy branch, cocking his arm like he would hold a cricket bat and tensing his muscles. The next moment the constable passed in front of him.

Sweeney swung the branch as hard as he could. The blow caught the constable on the forehead and knocked him unconscious, splitting his forehead open and sending a stream of blood coursing across his face.

Sweeney stood for a moment considering what to do next and then quickly decided. He unbuttoned the constable's jacket and flipped him over to get the jacket off him. Then he yanked off the man's uniform pants. Sweeney quickly shed his own jacket and trousers and dressed in the policeman's uniform. As the finishing touch, he picked up the constable's uniform cap, which had been sent flying into the bushes when he struck the man. Not a perfect fit, he thought, but it will have to do. Sweeney ran his hands down the sides of the jacket to smooth it out and then turned to the west, toward the wall that bordered the edge of the woods.

இ

Bradnum edged carefully into the thick foliage, keeping a hand in front of his face to prevent his eyes from being stabbed by low branches. He had gone about two hundred feet when he stopped suddenly. The sound of someone hurrying through the trees was cut short by a wet-sounding thwack and then the thud of something, or someone, hitting the ground.

He stood silently with an ear cocked toward the area from where the sound had come. He could hear the sound of water running over rocks, but over it was a scuffling sound. Bradnum made up his mind to approach cautiously.

The ground sloped away slightly and Bradnum moved gingerly across a small brook, trying to keep his boots dry by hopping across from stone to stone. On the other side he saw the tracks where others had climbed the soft bank. Withdrawing the small revolver from his jacket pocket, Bradnum climbed the bank and continued on toward a large elm tree that had been blown down.

As Bradnum moved around the uprooted tree, he saw a man's silhouette and raised the pistol, cocking the hammer back.

"Hold on there. Put up your hands."

As soon as the words were out of his mouth, Bradnum realized he had made a mistake and had one of his own constables at gunpoint. He thumbed the hammer down and lowered the pistol.

"Never mind. Put your hands down. Have you seen him?" Bradnum said stepping closer.

As he did, his toe caught on the body on the ground. In the same instant, the man in the constable's uniform whirled around and grabbed his gun hand, twisting his wrist back toward his forearm.

A searing pain shot up Bradnum's arm and he involuntarily dropped the pistol.

Sweeney snatched the pistol and thumbed back the hammer, pointing the muzzle directly at Bradnum's chest.

"Bloody busy day, wouldn't you say?" he asked.

Bradnum shut his eyes and lowered his chin, waiting for the shot. It didn't come. He opened his eyes to see Sweeney smiling at him.

"No, Mate. I think you'll be of more use to me if you're breathing. You see, you're going to help me out of these woods."

"I will not help you escape." Bradnum thrust his chest out in defiance.

"You either come with me or else you can have a bullet in the brain now. Your choice." Sweeney pointed the revolver at the middle of Bradnum's forehead. "Which is it?"

Bradnum heaved a sigh. "Which way?"

Chapter Twenty-four

Bradnum winced as Sweeney jammed the revolver's muzzle into his back.

"Come on, Mate. Pick up the pace a bit. We want to get out of here before dark," Sweeney said, pushing the muzzle deeper into his back.

Bradnum took a deep breath and looked back over his shoulder. "You should know you won't get away with this. You will be stopped. And probably hanged."

Sweeney laughed. "By who? You boyos haven't been able to catch me so far and it's only been bloody bad luck that you got this close to me today. Hold on now." Sweeney clamped his hand on Bradnum's shoulder and pulled him to a stop.

Twenty feet away stood a thick iron fence, five feet high and topped by pointed spikes, discouraging anyone but the most motivated individual from climbing over it. Sweeney pushed Bradnum forward until they were close enough to touch the warm metal.

"All right, Mate. Up and over you go," Sweeney said, gesturing with the revolver.

"How do you expect me to get over those spikes?"

Sweeney shook his head as if he were dealing with a backward child. "There's plenty o' room between the spikes for you to get handholds and footholds if you're careful. If you're not, then I might have to find some other way to get through the cordon you've put around the estate." He looked Bradnum up and down. "Let's be at it, shall we? I haven't got all bloody afternoon."

Bradnum looked from Sweeney to the top of the iron fence. Damn, he thought. The buggar was going to get away and there seemed to be nothing he could do about it. Unless...

Bradnum grabbed a cross-piece on the fence and pulled himself up to the top, slipping his right foot in between two spikes. He slid his free hand in the slot between two other spikes and pushed himself over the top, landing awkwardly on the other side and sitting down hard on his butt.

"Well done, Inspector," Sweeney said with a laugh. "Now you sit right there and wait for me to get over. And no tricks, mind you." He waved the revolver at Bradnum. With the quickness of a cat going after an unsuspecting bird, Sweeney hauled himself up and over the iron fence, landing feet first with a thud.

"Let's move, Mate. On your feet."

Bradnum rose slowly and headed west again, parting bushes and weeds as he passed through a dense section of scrub brush. He stole a glance behind him and saw that Sweeney was lagging behind. At a dip in the forest floor, Bradnum stumbled, seemingly by accident, and grabbed at his ankle, rolling around in the dirt.

"What's all this rubbish?" Sweeney said, moving close to Bradnum and peering close to where he held his ankle.

As Sweeney leaned over him, Bradnum released his grip and kicked upward with all his strength. The toe of his boot caught Sweeney under the chin and sent him sprawling backwards, his arms outstretched and the revolver flying 15 feet away. He landed with a crunch on his back.

Bradnum sprang forward, scrabbling on his hands and knees across the soft earth until he had the butt of the revolver in his hand. He turned and pointed it at Sweeney, but only saw Sweeney's back disappearing through the thick brush. Bradnum aimed carefully, but then lowered the pistol. Damn. He didn't have a shot.

&

Think! Where did the road that bordered the woods go? Bradnum pictured the map on his office table and saw the looping belly of the woods jutting out from the edge of the estate toward the west. It bulged outward and was bordered a narrow dirt road. Sweeney would certainly head for the road, he thought. Bradnum pushed himself up from the dirt and began to dog-trot through the thinning underbrush, intent on intercepting Sweeney on the road.

Five minutes later Bradnum burst through a particularly thick stand of bushes and stumbled into a shallow ditch alongside a dirt road. The trickle of water in the ditch's bottom was cool on his hands and Bradnum scooped water into his mouth, slurping greedily. He lay hidden in the ditch for several minutes before he heard footsteps crunching on the gravel imbedded in the road. Could it be Sweeney? It must be, he thought. He couldn't imagine anyone else traveling the estate road right now.

Bradnum reached into his jacket pocket and pulled out the revolver, leaving the hammer down for the moment. He tensed and waited for the sound of the footsteps to pass above him and then sprang through the light bushes and onto the road.

Sweeney jumped back from Bradnum's attack, grabbing Bradnum's shoulder and the muzzle of the revolver pointed at him. As Bradnum thumbed back the hammer, Sweeney twisted the revolver, forcing its muzzle toward the sky, where it discharged with a loud report and a puff of cordite smoke.

Bradnum's attention was fixed on the revolver at the moment of its firing and Sweeney used this distraction to knee him in the groin. Bradnum fell to the ground writhing, gripping on his private parts and dropping the revolver. He watched through tear-filled eyes as Sweeney picked up the heavy revolver and then flinched as Sweeny smashed it against the side of his head. The world went black.

❧

Bradnum opened his eyes to see cumulus clouds drifting above him, hinting at the rain that had seemed sure to come earlier in the day. He started to sit up, but his head buzzed and he fell back, bouncing his skull off the gravel roadway. He reached back and massaged his head. Damn, he thought. I've lost him again. He pushed himself into a sitting position and had to wait a full minute for the dizzy spell to subside. Bradnum looked up and down the road, but saw no sign of a living soul. Sweeney was gone.

Forcing himself to his feet, he looked back at the forest he had come through earlier and shook his head. There was no way that he could negotiate the woods in his condition. He touched his temple and his hand came away stained with blood. He would have to walk the road to summon help and then organize a search party for Sweeney.

Ten minutes later, Bradnum approached Elmfield House's entry gate as two troopers snapped to attention.

"I want assistance here," Bradnum said, stumbling toward them.

The younger sentry leaped forward and grabbed him under his arms, helping him into the gatehouse.

"Here you are, sir. Sit here. Let me get you some water."

The sentry returned with a mug of cool water and handed it to Bradnum, who drank greedily, spilling rivulets down the side of his chin.

"I must speak to the captain in charge of the detail," he began, puffing to catch his breath. "The assassin has slipped away from me."

"Looks as if he got the better of you, sir," the older sentry said.

Bradnum fixed the sentry with a stare. "Get on to the captain and have him report to me with a dozen men. We have to put out a cordon to catch this man."

The sentry hesitated, but then saluted smartly. "Right away, sir."

Bradnum turned to the younger sentry. "I want you to help me to the main house. I must see the king and the president immediately."

The sentry's eyes widened. "Sir, I am not to leave my post. The gate would be unguarded."

"That should not be your concern at the moment. First you must get me to the main house. Then return to your duties."

The young sentry seemed on the verge of refusing, but finally shrugged his shoulders. "Anything you say, sir. Let me help you up."

Inside Elmfield House's entry hall, Bradnum straightened up and brushed specks of dirt and bits of leaves from his trouser legs and jacket. Within a few minutes, the king emerged down the hall and walked up to him.

"You are unharmed, I am told."

"Yes, your majesty. But I've come to ascertain your safety and that of the president."

"We're fine. I just left Theodore holding a losing hand at whist." A wide smile split the king's face and he leaned closer. "I must win back the cost of the case of Dom Perignon, eh?"

"I must request that your majesty and President Roosevelt remain here tonight so my men can protect you. I understand the president leaves tomorrow for Africa."

"That is correct," the king said, stroking his beard. "I'll finish him off at whist and then release him."

Bradnum bowed and turned to leave.

"One more thing, Inspector. Be sure you catch this man. What's his name?"

Bradnum turned back to face the king. "Patrick Sweeney, your Majesty. And make no mistake; catching him is precisely what I plan on doing."

❧

Bradnum snatched off his hat and sailed it across his office, bouncing it off an oak bookcase. He dropped into his desk chair and sighed loudly. "Damn it, Glew. Why can't we lay our hands on this man? We've been so close."

Glew shrugged his shoulders. "Maybe we should try thinking more like he does."

Bradnum's eyes popped widely and he sat forward bouncing his belly against the edge of the desk. "That's a smashing idea. Do you have something specific in mind?" He indicated a chair at the side of the desk and Glew sat.

"Well, sir, it's like this. If I was this bloke trying to get away, I'd want to get away as fast as possible, like a train."

"That's a solid assumption, Glew, but hardly news to us. And we have men posted at the main terminal and the goods depot."

"Yes sir, but I wasn't finished." At a nod from Bradnum, Glew continued. "As I was saying, Inspector, the man may want to get out of town quickly, but he's not shown us the usual criminal stupidity so far. I thought he might be looking for a fast, but quieter way to leave."

Bradnum stared at Glew, practically willing him to hurry with his thoughts. "And that way might be what?"

Glew stuck a finger in his collar and pulled the fabric away from his throat. "I was thinking he might slip away from us by taking a steamer from one of the wharves. There's plenty of them available at the docks."

Bradnum continued staring at Glew for a full half-minute while the beginnings of an idea took shape. Suddenly, he slapped the desk with a loud smack and leaned back in his chair. "Of course, you're right. And I think I know the steamer line where we can find Sweeney."

Glew blinked as if he had been blinded by a bright light. "You do?"

"Yes, I do. I think that Sweeney will not give up. He'll be at the wharf that the president will use to depart for Africa." Bradnum leaned forward. "Now let me tell you what I want you to do."

Patrick Sweeney slowly opened the door to the dim room and locked it behind him. He looked around the small, rundown room and clucked his tongue. How far I've come, he thought. But it should be over by tomorrow. And then the cause will be taken up in America.

He reached under the stained mattress and pulled a satchel from under the bed frame. Sweeney held each item up for inspection as he removed them: a longish, brown beard, a shapeless dark hat, a pair of spectacles with glass instead of lenses, a long black coat and a pair of false eyebrows that reminded him of wooly caterpillars. He smoothed down the hairs of the beard and smiled, then reached into the satchel and removed a map of Hull's docks.

Spreading the map out of the bed, Sweeney knelt at the bed's edge and ran a finger along the wharfs, from west to east. First the Victoria dock, surrounded by timber yards and a half tide basin. Next was St. Andrew's Dock and its extension, stretched out hard along the Humber.

Sweeney rolled his shoulders to ease the tension and then bent back to the map. Warehouses and a graving dock surrounded the William Wright Dock, and finally his finger traced a line into the Albert Dock, with its Riverside Quay and steamship departure terminal at the far end of town where a spit of land thrust into the Humber.

Sweeney pursed his lips and looked more closely at the warehouses surrounding the Albert Dock and the approaches to the Riverside Quay. He would have to be careful because there were only two exits from the quay. If the police had both of them guarded, it would be mighty difficult to get onto the quay and perhaps near impossible to get out. Sweeney stood and smiled. He'd beaten the police so far. No reason to doubt himself now.

He spread open the leather satchel and reached inside, withdrawing a clump of six sticks of dynamite tied together, and set them alongside the false eyebrows. Next to the dynamite, he put the fuses and quick match. Sweeney stood back and put his hands on his hips, staring at the array of material on the bed. Roosevelt was as good as dead, he thought.

@hapter Twenty-five

The two-story Riverside Quay Station could only be approached from two directions because the structure was sandwiched in between the wide expanse of the Albert Dock to the north and the Humber's channel to the south. From the west, the station approach road dead-ended at a footbridge that stretched over a half-dozen railway sidings before dropping down along uncovered metal stairs to the concrete-decked quay. From the east, a carriage road ran along the seawall and terminated at the station.

Riverside Quay Station itself had seen better days, Bradnum thought, as he stood on the quay surveying the building. To his far right were the ticketing agent's office, a baggage room, a warren of small rooms serving as offices and private sitting rooms, and a large hall where passengers and visitors could await the departure of a ship. A storage area stood in the center of the structure, while a series of interconnected rooms took up the west side of the building, occupied by customs officials, baggage porters, stevedores, the stationmaster and the chief ticketing agent's crew.

Bradnum turned to Glew and scrutinized his appearance. Glew was dressed in a ticketing agent's blue uniform jacket, blue trousers, white shirt and a billed cap that carried the silver badge of the North Star Steamship Line. Bradnum brushed a speck of lint from Glew's shoulder.

"I'm sure I don't have to tell you how important a job you have. You are the first line of defense against Sweeney and one of the few people who can identify the man. I've arranged to have you seemingly working alongside the managing ticket agent so you can raise the alarm when Sweeney shows up."

"Why do you think that he'll come to the ticketing agent?"

"Actually, it's quite simple. If he wants to get close to the president, he will have to mingle in with the other passengers and appear as they do. That means he should visit the ticketing agent to get a ticket for his passage and then make himself scarce in the waiting hall or in one of the private rooms. That is how we shall nab him."

"What if he sees what we're up to?"

"He shouldn't, even though he's a crafty one. Besides a token number of uniformed police at strategic spots along the quay and in the station, I also have ten men in civilian clothes placed throughout the building and near the approaches. Once Sweeney walks into our trap, I can't see how he can get out."

After he sent Glew to the ticket agent's office, Bradnum cast a long look at the ends of the quay. Passengers had started to arrive from both directions and queue for tickets. Some had moved into the waiting hall, while porters pushed steel-wheeled carts laden with bags, leather luggage and trunks down the quay toward baggage storage. It was time to make himself scarce. He didn't want Sweeney to see him and make a run for it.

ঌ

Sweeney squared his shoulders and then rolled them forward to approximate a stooped semblance. The black frock coat he wore hung midway down his calves, covering black trousers and boots. Atop his head he wore a battered black hat of the type favored by Jewish rabbis. His long beard, held in place with gum arabic, spread wildly across the front of his neck and chest, complimented by a pair of graying, bushy eyebrows. Perched on the end of his nose were a pair of brass-rimmed spectacles that only he knew contained nothing but clear glass in the eyepieces. He carried a black leather satchel with a large silver Star of David painted on it.

Sweeney paid the carriage driver and shuffled along the station approach until he reached the end of the ticket queue. A porter approached him.

"Do ye have any other luggage, rabbi?"

Sweeney turned to the man and smiled. "It has already been delivered to your storeroom, my son. Thank you for your offer of assistance."

The porter moved down the line and Sweeney shuffled forward, arriving at the head of the line a few minutes later. As the couple in front of him stepped forward, he caught a glimpse of a man in an agent's uniform who was out of place. It was the policeman who chased him at the dedication ceremony.

When his turn came, he approached the barred window and slid his money through the grating. His stoop was more pronounced now and his voice cracked with age. "Out to Le Havre," he said. "No return."

He saw the policeman look him over and then turn away, obviously unconcerned. The ticket agent slid a long printed ticket toward him. "Stand ready, rabbi. We expect to begin boarding passengers within the hour."

Sweeney nodded and smiled, and shuffled away from the window, heading toward the center of the building. But instead of entering the station through the large swinging doors of the waiting hall, he bypassed them and strolled toward the west end of the station, looking into office windows as he passed. At the extreme end of the station, a policeman stood watching him approach.

"May I help you, rabbi?"

"No thank you. I am only getting a last feel of the land before the slipping and sliding of the ship."

"Ah, I know what you mean," the policeman said. "The wife and me took a steamer across the channel last year in choppy water and I thought I'd never be the same again."

"Is something special happening here today?" Sweeney asked.

"What makes you think so?"

"There seem to be a number of policeman around," Sweeney replied, stroking his beard.

"Aye, it's because of the president leaving for Africa. He's due any time now. We've got a special room set aside for him so he won't be bothered by the citizens." The policeman inclined his head to the side toward the office behind him.

"Where would be a good spot for me to stand to get a glimpse of him when he arrives? I wasn't able to see him at his other appearances in town."

The policeman looked left and right before smiling at Sweeney. "Rabbi, anywhere along here will be fine. We'll be secluding him in the customs officer's office back there." He cocked his head again. "The president will have to come right along here to get to the office."

"Thanks for your advice, young man. I shall take up a post back there and await his appearance." Sweeney shuffled away in his stoop shouldered posture, tightly gripping the satchel. Damn, that was easy, he thought.

Thirty feet away he glimpsed over his shoulder and saw the policeman engaged in conversation with another citizen. Sweeney veered to the left and slipped through an unlocked door into the adjacent room. It was empty. Dropping the stooped pose, he moved to the back wall and cracked open the door there. Another empty office, but one with two exits. He stepped in and shut the door with a gentle click.

Sweeney slowly edged the west door ajar and peered through the crack. Empty. They must have cleared out all these offices as a safety precaution, he thought. He quickly entered and dead bolted the door behind him.

The customs officer's office was the next room west of where he stood. Setting his satchel on the floor at the base of the adjoining door, Sweeney snapped the clasp open and withdrew six sticks of dynamite wrapped tightly together along with a length of fuse. He wedged the dynamite against the foot of the door and then used his knife to perforate the end of one of the red tubes. Reaming the thin blade back and forth in the powder created a channel into which he threaded the fuse. Then he ran the fuse along the base of the wall to the rear door and cut the fuse at that point.

He checked the room behind him and found it empty too. A rear door led to an alleyway that ran in front of a long, low warehouse. The west end of the station was about 60 feet away and the footbridge another 200 feet from there. He bolted the door and returned to the room where he had laid the dynamite. Now he would have to wait.

A half hour later Sweeney became aware of a murmur running through the crowd on the quay outside. Within minutes, he heard cheering and applause, as a low roar went up from the crowd.

Roosevelt did not tarry outside, because the next thing Sweeney heard was the president being greeted in the room next door. Some North Star line official was going on and on about what an honor it was to have the president on board his ship. Sweeney shut out the sounds from next door and dug into his satchel for a match. It flared as he struck it, but he had been too strong and it went out. Sweeney held out his hand, fingers splayed and saw them trembling. Settle down, Boyo, he thought. You'll be out of here in a minute.

He withdrew another match and snapped its tip with his fingernail. Sweeney smiled as the match burst into flame and he inhaled the sulfurous fumes deeply. Then he touched the match to the end of the fuse, which sputtered brightly to life.

❧

Bradnum moved into the next empty office at the rear of the station. He had made a methodical search of the rooms adjacent to the president's location and come up empty. Perhaps Sweeney had decided that one more try at the president was pushing his luck. One more room to check, he thought, pushing the south door open. As he did, the door struck Sweeney in the back and sent him sprawling onto the floor.

Bradnum took in the scene of the rabbi, the black leather satchel and the quick fuse burning along the base of the wall. As he turned toward the wall to snatch at the burning fuse, Sweeney punched him flush on the side of the chin, bringing tears to his eyes and sending him crashing through the doorway and into the back office. Sweeney was on him instantly, pulling him up by the torso and smashing him in the face. Then he tightened his meaty hands on Bradnum's neck and the world went black.

❧

Bradnum awakened to a burning sensation and clapped his hand to the back of his neck. His hand quickly burned too and he sat bolt upright, bringing on a wave of nausea. The south wall between the two offices was in shambles and a fire burned brightly in the location where the bomb had exploded. The bomb room had been turned into rubble, blowing down the walls and opening a huge, jagged hole in the roof of the station. Looking up, Bradnum could see patches of blue sky through the smoke from the fire.

He pushed pieces of the wall planking off his legs and felt his face for wounds. There was a lump the size of an egg on his forehead and blood had covered his right eye so that he looked through a thin veil of red.

As Bradnum tried to stand, Glew pushed through the damaged rear door and caught him under the arms.

"Inspector, let's get you out of here."

"The president. Is he safe?"

"Yes. When the officers with him heard the commotion next door, they hustled him out of the building and onto the ship. That's when the bomb exploded. Gawd, what a fireball. You're lucky to still have your skin."

"The rabbi. What happened to the rabbi? It was Sweeney."

"The only rabbi I saw today was purchasing a ticket. You mean that was Sweeney?"

"It must have been. What a wonderful disguise. It's no wonder we all were taken in." Bradnum coughed up a wad of phlegm and spit it onto the charred floor. "Get me out of here and then get the men organized and searching for the rabbi. And remember, he's dangerous."

Sweeney melted into the crowd pouring over the footbridge toward the quay roadway, moving faster than he had previously when he adopted the stooped walk. No need for much secrecy now, he thought. Best to get far away from the quay.

Carriages and cabs were lined up along the end of the roadway, taking on full loads of passengers who were trying to get away from the scene of the explosion. Spotting a small shed at the side of a warehouse, Sweeney swiftly got inside, dropped his hat and stripped off his long black coat. Underneath he wore a pair of workman's coveralls. He pulled the false eyebrows off and then stripped off the beard, rubbing his face vigorously with the coat to remove the gum arabic.

Back outside, Sweeney walked farther along the row of carriages until he found one with an open seat. Motor cabs and horse drawn carriages were pulling out of line and jockeying for position before moving quickly west along road. As he pulled himself up into the open carriage, Sweeney looked back at the quay. He could just make out a uniformed man half-carrying another man from the back of the station. Sweeney took his seat just as the carriage driver snapped the reins and the cab lurched forward along the quay road toward town. He pulled a deep breath and tipped his hat to the driver. "God bless, all here," he said, smiling.

Alan M. Petrillo is a Tucson, Arizona-based journalist; the author of several books on historical military firearms; and the author of historical mysteries: *Full Moon*, and the first novel in the Victorian Carriage mystery series, *Asylum Lane.*

Visit the other mysteries:
     www.VictorianCarriageSeries.com
Call on Al in his author's parlour:
     www.AlanMPetrillo.com

35472523R00141

Made in the USA
San Bernardino, CA
24 June 2016